Worldwide consumption of bottled water has undergone phenomenal growth since the 1970s. This massive shift toward bottled water requires ever-increasing numbers of plastic containers, heightens impacts related to long-distance transportation, and contributes to polluting the planet's natural water sources.

Nearly 60 percent of all packaging is made for food and beverages. The global market for packaging is estimated at $500 billion, with a growth rate of 4 percent per year.

The dramatic increase in plastic packaging, single-use disposable food containers, and shopping bags, collectively known as "white pollution," has prompted increasing numbers of Asian cities and national governments to impose bans on certain types of disposable packaging.

PAPERORPLASTIC

Searching for Solutions to an Overpackaged World

Daniel Imhoff

A Watershed Media Book

Sierra Club Books

San Francisco

Published by Sierra Club Books
85 Second Street, San Francisco, CA 94105
www.sierraclub.org/books

Produced and distributed by
University of California Press
Berkeley and Los Angeles, California
University of California Press, Ltd.
London, England
www.ucpress.edu

Library of Congress Cataloging-in-Publication Data available upon request from the publisher.

Photo Credits

All photographs copyright © Roberto Carra, except as listed below.
Page i and back cover: Mountain of cans, Republic of Korea, © K. Kang/ UNEP/Peter Arnold, Inc.
Pages ii–iii: Boys collecting floating waste, Manila Bay, Republic of the Philippines, © Hartmut Schwarzbach/UNEP/Peter Arnold, Inc.
Pages iv–v: Lovers among discarded cans, The Netherlands, © Siebe Vriend/UNEP/Peter Arnold, Inc.
Pages vi–vii: Woman sorting plastic bags, Katmandu, Nepal, © Mark Edwards/Peter Arnold, Inc.
Page viii and back cover: Boys among plastic bottles, Republic of the Philippines, © J. Tanodra/UNEP/Peter Arnold, Inc.
Page 8: Clearcut in British Columbia, © Gary Braasch
Page 9: Cleaning up oil spill, Prince William Sound, Alaska, © Bob Hallinen/*Anchorage Daily News*
Page 23: Dam, courtesy of International Rivers Network
Page 33: World Bottle, courtesy of Heineken International
Page 59: Printers on pallets, © Kevin Howard
Pages 64 and 139: Eco-Pint ice cream containers, reprinted with permission from Ben & Jerry's
Page 94: FSC certification stamp, courtesy of Forest Stewardship Council
Page 97 and back cover: FSC-certified brewery pallets, © Phillip Guillery, Dovetail Partners
Page 103: Mill, courtesy of Durango-McKinley
Page 117: Cornfield, courtesy of U.S. Department of Agriculture
Pages 124–125: Windmills, Ringkoebing Fjord, Denmark, © Hartmut Schwarzbach/Peter Arnold, Inc.
Page 134: FSC-certified wood pallet, courtesy of Forest Stewardship Council
Page 136: Lightweight Ecobottle, courtesy of Sarda Acque Minerali
Page 138: Refillable beer bottle, courtesy of Veltins International; pelicans, Corel's Professional Photography
Page 139: Reverse vending machine, courtesy of TOMRA
Page 140: Aveda packaging, © Daniel Imhoff; wax-free fresh pack (also on back cover), courtesy of Newark Group
Page 141: Refill station, courtesy of Restore Products
Page 142: Wooden produce boxes, © Barbara Damrosch
Page 143: Tea canister, © 2002, Polara Studios; "Buy Fresh/Buy Local" graphics, courtesy of Food Routes; fleece jacket, reprinted with permission from Patagonia
Page 144: Toothbrush, © Daniel Imhoff; pasta tin, © Daniel Imhoff; owl box production, © Steve Simmons; baby barn owls, © Steve Simmons
Page 145: Thanksgiving Coffee foil pouch, courtesy of Chris Blum; mail-order garment package, © Daniel Imhoff

Printed in Canada on New Leaf acid-free papers. Pages 1–136 and 145–168 are printed on Ecobook 60, which contains 60 percent post-consumer waste, processed chlorine free. Pages i–viii and 137–144 are printed on Reincarnation Matte, which is archivally coated and contains a minimum of 50 percent post-consumer waste, processed chlorine free.

ISBN 1-57805-117-7
First Edition
08 07 06 05
10 9 8 7 6 5 4 3 2 1

ACKNOWLEDGMENTS

No book is produced in a vacuum. One of the earliest fruits of our fifteen-year writing and photography collaboration was a humorous video about office recycling. This particular work has been years in the making and has benefitted from the help of numerous individuals. Anne Chick's extensive research and case studies graced this book with depth and international scope. Rod Miller's fact-finding provided a solid understanding of packaging's environmental impacts. Leda Huta authored an early piece on wood reduction and offered her unflagging support throughout. Heartfelt thanks to Randy Hayes, Janine M. Benyus, Dayna Baumeister, Jerry Mander, and Simon Retallack for their contributions to the text. Thanks also to Brian Dougherty of Celery Design Collaborative for a study of ink toxicity. The Resource lists were prepared by Wendy Jedlicka and edited by Emmett Hopkins, Dawnelise Regnery, and Christen Crumley. For peer-reviewing and editing we were fortunate to work with Marissa Juhler, Warren Karlenzig, Erin Johnson, Julia Zafferano, and John Delfausse. We are grateful to Medea Minnich for her indexing and to David Van Ness for his pre-production computer expertise. Many thanks to our publishing partners: Helen Sweetland and Danny Moses of Sierra Club Books and Anna Bullard of University of California Press. We are greatly indebted to the foundations that have assisted us throughout the publication of Watershed Media's entire Wood Reduction Trilogy: The Garfield Foundation, Richard and Rhoda Goldman Foundation, Forest Trends, Giles W. and Elise G. Mead Foundation, Laird Norton Endowment Foundation, Turner Foundation, and Weeden Foundation. Thanks to Chris Blum for help with our title and to the board of Watershed Media. And last but by no means least, to Quincey Tompkins Imhoff and Claudia Carra for their incalculable contributions and support—*grazie mille*. Perhaps, in some small way, we are all helping to shine a light where it is so desperately needed.

—Dan Imhoff and Roberto Carra
Watershed Media
January 2005

We also wish to thank:

The Biomimicry Institute
Peter Buckley
Mark Buell and Susie Tompkins Buell
Jennie Curtis
Jib Ellison
Greg Gale
The Green Business Letter

Greg Hendrickson
Kevin Howard
Diana Donlon Karlenzig
Bill Orts
Carl Rabago
Raymond Communications
Rick Reed

Mark Ritchie
Paul Russell
Mike Stone
Anne Telford
Kate White

CONTENTS

The Right Stuff: Reenvisioning Waste and Our Future

I have spent much of my life fighting to make the world's last undeveloped natural places safe for the indigenous peoples and native species that inhabit them. My journey has taken me to the mighty Amazon and deep into the darkest reaches of Borneo's rain forests. I can say from personal experience that it is just plain wrong for those cathedral forests to fall for throwaway transport pallets, packaging fiber, or oil feedstock to make plastic wrappers. Back at home, at the top of the consumption chain, it tortures my soul to see the incessant flow of packaging going into dead-end landfill: toxic cemeteries. Each piece thrown away pulls at the threads of the complex fabric of the natural world and contributes to the ultimate unraveling of our common future.

Because we are faced with pressing problems such as global climate destablization, total destruction of irreplaceable ecosystems, and widespread species extinction, you might think issues such as industrial and household packaging are low on the list of environmental priorities. But as this book correctly asserts, packaging is part and parcel of lifestyles that have become almost completely disconnected from earth's natural cycles and capacity to process our industrial wastes. The time has come to address what has become an absurdly overpackaged world.

By our very nature, we are traders. We require food, clothing, shelter, culture, and comforts, and packages help deliver them. To that end, we must establish systems that honorably and rationally support trade but at the same time protect natural systems and habitats from which all things are derived. It is equally important that we address manageable basic issues as well as the looming, daunting challenges. Doing so can inspire us to realize an ecologically sustainable society in our lifetime.

As an environmental commissioner for the city of San Francisco, I authored a resolution to achieve 75 percent waste diversion by 2010 and zero waste by 2020. In 2004, San Francisco will have surpassed 62 percent diversion of its waste flow—well on its way to meeting the first target and ultimately the second: no waste. This is the stuff, the right stuff, of creating a more sustainable world. Some may argue that energy spent recovering every last scrap of packaging is counterproductive and that, without complex systems and infrastructure in place, it is far more efficient just to bury our castoffs in the world's "wastelands." I'm not for wastelands, and I don't imagine you are either.

Here is a definition of sustainability that might surprise you: Diverse and rewarding lifestyles that many would want to emulate, and if they all did, the planet's natural systems and wildlife populations would flourish, increasingly, each generation. This is a vision of not only a better world but also one with a conscious, self-healing capacity. However, if we are to save our ancient rain forests and build the better world that we know is possible, we need your help now. We all have a part to play.

Envision a zero-waste society, one in which consumer goods and the packaging that wraps them are no longer repositories of spent energy and materials. Those sacred materials feed new jobs, new forms of economic development, and new durable goods. Now imagine a society powered by 100 percent renewable energy. Imagine it in less than 25 years as is the policy and plan for both San Francisco and Oakland, California. Next, quadruple the carrying capacity of mass transit. Then, transform chemical-laden, erosion-prone agribusiness into organic, soil-building systems that provide a steady supply of healthy food that is better for both people and the planet. This is sustainability in action. This is the ecologically evolved society where you, your family, and future generations deserve to live.

Transforming our packaging systems is a necessary part of that vision, not just through simple materials substitution or the incremental changes of eco-efficiency, but through the deeper systems approach that you will learn about in this book. Remember, waste is a construct that humanity invented at a time when industry lacked a deep understanding of ecological processes. There is no waste in nature.

Paper or Plastic is the final installment in Watershed Media's Wood Reduction Trilogy, which includes *The Guide to Tree-Free, Recycled, and Certified Papers* and *Building with Vision*. These books tackle the difficult task of addressing the impacts of increasing wood consumption with on-the-ground solutions for our design trades.

For Dan Imhoff, Roberto Carra, and myself, these books have been an outgrowth of our love and respect for the world's ancient forests and the creatures that abound there. As we all know, the highest "use" of an old forest is as an old forest— providing nesting sites for fluorescent-beaked toucans as well as a canopied highway for bands of red howler monkeys to scamper about. And we can't forget the role forests play in providing all life with clean air, clean water, and a stable climate. By reducing wood-fiber consumption—moving from throwaway to closed-loop recyclable and reusable distribution systems—we can move toward a future of healthy forests rather than continue the desperate fight to prevent their destruction. In order to help toucans and howler monkeys keep their glorious homes, we can and we must dramatically reduce the amount of virgin wood logged from ancient and intact forests for use in paper, construction, and packaging. This book and its companions are an important step on that essential journey.

—Randy Hayes
President of Rainforest Action Network
and Sustainability Director for the
City of Oakland

Clearcut hillside in British Columbia. Canada is a major supplier of pulpwood for the paper industry.

THE PACKAGING

"Paper or plastic?" This seemingly innocuous question assumed almost existential dimensions during the early 1990s, as it became a daily reminder to most of us that our industrial consumer society (in a world approaching six billion people) was running a collision course with the planet's ecological life-support systems. The query was innocent enough, attempting to narrow a dilemma of immense complexity into a simple choice between materials. Do we clearcut forests, grind them to chips, and pulp and bleach them with chlorine-based compounds (generating carcinogenic byproducts) to make boxes, bags, and to-go cups primarily for one-time use? Or do we make a pact with demon hydrocarbon, refining ancient sunlight into lightweight, easily compactible bottles, wraps, and foams?

A decade later, there is still no general consensus about the environmental preferability of choosing paper versus plastic. Wood-based packaging and petroleum-based plastics (and their sidekicks, glass, aluminum, steel, and combinations thereof) all have their environmental transgressions and economic justifications, and must be considered on a case-by-case basis. Wood is theoretically a renewable resource, but only theoretically. Global forestry practices are so

Workers pressure-washing a beach in the aftermath of the 1989 Exxon Valdez oil spill in Alaska.

LANDSCAPE

rapidly degrading forest ecosystems that a vast amount of the world's biodiversity may be lost within the half century as a result of paper, building, packaging, and other products. Plastic is recyclable depending on the resin type(s) and whether local systems exist to reuse, recover, and reprocess them. But, though two plastic types (HDPE and PET) achieve relatively high reuse and recovery rates in some countries, overall plastic packaging recycling remains abysmally low. In fact, the current trend is toward layering different plastic materials into single-use "smart" packages, making recycling impossible or economically impractical. Also, the

manufacturing and incineration of some plastics, such as polyvinyl chloride (PVC), are so toxic that many experts argue that they should be banned outright.

Because packaging has rapidly become an integral part of how all of us meet our daily needs, it serves as an easy scapegoat for a world bursting at the seams. Although dwarfed by many complex and urgent environmental problems, packaging is a visible and persistent feature on the physical landscape. About one-third of the gross weight and half of the volume of America's municipal solid-waste stream is composed of packaging materials[1]—at least 300 pounds per person per year. That figure includes a half billion virgin-wood transportation pallets that are used only once and sent to landfills—enough material on a volume basis to frame 300,000 houses.[2] Yet despite negative attention in the mainstream media, packaging remains in a growth phase. A study by the Grass Roots Recycling Network reported that, between 1990 and 1997, plastic packaging grew five times faster by weight than plastic recovered for recycling.[3] Riding the economic boom of the 1990s, U.S. production capacity of paperboard folding cartons used to box everything from carryout food to pharmaceuticals, breakfast cereals, and printer cartridges, increased by 30 percent.[4] Each year more than 150 billion single-use beverage containers are sold in the United States, not to mention a conservative estimate of 320 million hot and cold take-out cups purchased every day across the country.[5] Some 19 billion pounds of "peanuts" and 25 billion cups made from polystyrene compose just a fraction of the 1 million pounds of waste that author Paul Hawken estimates are generated on behalf of the average American each year.[6] One might even say that a tendency toward overpackaging is inextricably ingrained in our culture, psyche, and economy. This is never more evident than during the holiday season, when waste output spikes 25 percent in the United States. A CNN poll TV-broadcast in December 2001 reported that 80 percent of people surveyed bought Christmas gifts for their pets—and that 67 percent wrapped them! A number of developing countries are also beginning to follow our

lead. China, for example, is rapidly becoming the world's largest market for disposable plastic and containers, now known as "white garbage."[7]

There is no doubt that packaging fulfills invaluable functions in a global economy that provides basic necessities as well as consumer and commercial goods to billions of people every day. Modern packaging's essential services—product protection, transportation, convenience, safety, hygiene, nutrition, spoilage prevention, information, branding, merchandising, theft-proofing, and regulatory compliance—are widely acknowledged. These services should not be underestimated. If a package fails to safely and adequately deliver its product, even more resources can be squandered.

Packaging falls into three main categories: primary, secondary, and transport packages.

● **Primary packages.** This type of packaging—from beer bottle to ice cream tub—contains the actual product. Primary packs sometimes employ multiple layers, materials, or impermeable coatings to accomplish their task.

● **Secondary packages.** In effect, these package the primary package, sometimes using additional layers or materials to seal out moisture. This could be something as simple as a box of tea bags wrapped in a sheath of cellophane, or a shrinkwrapped case of four six-packs of bottled water. Together, the primary and secondary packages constitute the product delivery system.

● **Transport or tertiary packages.** These packages carry products in their primary and secondary packaging. They can have several elements, including corrugated cartons, shock-absorbing filler materials, bulk carriers (such as wooden pallets), strapping, shrink-wrapping, returnable plastic containers, and so on.

Some experts question just how critical the "packaging problem" really is. Both the upstream and the downstream effects of packaging production and disposal certainly pale in comparison to the devastating impacts of escalating resource extraction and energy consumption. The increasing use of coal as an energy source, the proliferation of the automobile, and the expansion of industrial agriculture all relegate packaging to the back burner of the world's environmental ills.

To view packaging in a broader perspective, 70 percent of the total nonenergy resource consumption in the United States is targeted toward the construction industries and infrastructure development; packaging represents just a portion of the remaining 30 percent.[8] In many parts of the industrialized world, household packaging constitutes approximately one-third of the municipal solid-waste stream, which in turn accounts for approximately one-third of the total waste stream. So, in effect, household packaging contributes about 15 percent of the total waste burden. (Packaging's share of the total waste stream is significantly higher in the United States; see the graph on page 20.) In

addition, recycling is generally heralded as the optimal solution for the proliferation of household packaging. Yet depending on the recycling infrastructure and distances between collection sites and reprocessing facilities, it can sometimes cost more to sort, recover, and reprocess materials (economically as well as in terms of fossil-fuel and energy use) than simply to use virgin materials in the first place. To be fair, materials and recovery systems need to be assessed on a case-by-case basis.

Even while popular misconceptions and hotly debated interpretations may exist about both the extent of the packaging crisis and the necessary solutions, one thing remains clear: multiple factors support the need for more effective use of energy, materials, money, and human effort expended in all walks of life. Citizens and politicians around the world are increasingly reluctant to site new landfills, incinerators, paper mills, and other manufacturing plants in their communities. By the mid-1990s, nearly 60 percent of the annual $500 billion packaging industry was paper-based, meaning those materials at one time originated in forests.[9] Concerns about the safety of plasticizers, additives, and other "bad actors" released during the manufacture and incineration of plastics remain high. And, though one could argue that too much emphasis is placed on litter, improvements could certainly be made along every step of the "packaging chain"—by manufacturers, converters, designers, fillers, distributors, governments, and consumers.

The Package Is the Product

In its defense, the primary package can be seen as a means to an end, the last stage in a product's design that must be considered as an integral part of the product. The laws of modern retail design dictate that a primary package must accurately reflect its contents in order to achieve its ultimate goal— the repeat purchase. In the words of packaging design guru Primo Angeli, "A package has to feel real. The graphics can be aesthetically interesting, but if the potential buyer has to stop and think about surface design apart from the product, the purchase potential decreases. As in theater, when you are aware that an actor is acting, the spell is broken."[10]

For this reason, primary packaging has been called the "skin of commerce," because it both piques and simplifies the purchasing process. In the retail arena, packaging becomes multifunctional: the front man, the merchandiser, the protector, the delivery person. Bad-mouth the package, and you're merely shooting the messenger, the messenger that must be viewed in light of its many capacities within a complex global economy.

There is, however, a fine line between necessary and excess packaging. Single-use, small-portion, convenience packaging and other egregious examples of overpackaging seem to be escalating, not decreasing. Most of us experience such existential moments regularly, when, after unwrapping, cutting, or tearing into an urgently needed package, we are left holding the bag (literally) or wrapper, bottle, blister pack, or double cup. Then there is the universal frustration and rage that accompanies unpacking then picking up after a carton of Styrofoam peanuts many times the volume of what it protected.

Packaging manufacturers and industry insiders will tell us that they are merely supplying consumers with what we want. And to a great extent they are right. We are a world of increasingly sophisticated consumers living in an age of unprecedented material wealth and abundance. Convenience packaging saves invaluable preparation time in a society where meal preparation has fallen from 2.5 hours in 1930 to 15 minutes by 1990.[11] Jumbo clear packs in national chain stores prevent shoplifting and allow us to purchase in bulk at deep discounts. But there is another side as well. Packaging sells. At times packages sell so well that they might be considered predatory. (For example, what child can resist the lure of the individually packaged, interactive assortment in Lunchables? Yet what child might decline the clever merchandising if he or she knew that the package could negatively affect wildlife or that it might be the precursor of a lifetime of unhealthy dietary habits?) Using over-engineered materials, an excess of graphics, and other gimmicks are proven techniques that boost sales. The degree to which modern packaging serves marketing, branding, and sales interests rather than fulfilling the more essential functions of safety, efficiency, convenience, delivery, and environmental health and security deserves to be questioned. Writing about the life-cycle analysis of packaging, Frank Ackerman of the Department of Global Development and the Environment at Tufts University eloquently reasoned that just because packaging sells doesn't mean it is necessary:

> It is possible to believe both that some [packaging] is essential, and that the trend is still toward increasing waste in packaging. Waste could result from a competitive "arms race" in which one company adopts larger, more elaborate packaging solely to compete with another company's larger, more elaborate packaging, in the struggle to win the attention of consumers. Producers could misinterpret consumer acceptance of increasing levels of packaging as evidence of a desire for even more. Cost calculations could show that it is cheaper to use more packaging, while failing to recognize the environmental costs of packaging production and disposal. Any of these reasons could lead to a pyramid of growing waste rising on a foundation of socially useful roles for packaging.[12]

In addition to making consumption easier and more predictable, packaging allows us to reach beyond our local regions for sources of basic necessities, increasing both the distance and the disconnection between ourselves and the goods we consume. The single-use container is in fact a post–World War II phenomenon that has, among other things, helped to boost the distance that common produce travels from field to table. A study entitled "Food, Fuel, and Freeways," sponsored by the Leopold Center for Sustainable Agriculture, for example, showed that common produce items such as grapes, cauliflower, peas, broccoli, spinach, and lettuce now travel an average of more than 2,000 miles before reaching midwestern markets.[13] In addition to the vast miles that foods, animal feeds, and beverages of all kinds now journey, the shift from bulk to single-use containerization is not without significant resource impacts. A detailed study by the University of Michigan's Center for Sustainable Systems conducted for the New Hampshire–based Stonyfield Farm yogurt company found that bulk containers have far fewer impacts than smaller ones. "It takes more energy for a smaller cup on an ounce-per-ounce basis," Stonyfield Farm vice president of natural resources Nancy Hirshberg reported. "The amount of packaging used per unit of product is substantially more for smaller products.... If all Stonyfield Farm yogurt were sold in 32-ounce containers [instead of the predominant 8-ounce size], the actualized energy savings would be equivalent to 11,250 barrels of oil."[14] For this to be effective, however, consumers would also have to adjust their eating habits so that buying in bulk does not cause excess food to spoil.

Cooking Time

1930 **2 hrs. 30 min.**

1990 **15 min.**

The expected time to prepare a meal has plummeted since 1930.
Source: Food Marketing Institute, 1996.

Wading Upstream in the Waste Stream

An individual aluminum can, a #1 PET bottle, or a paperboard pizza box can serve as a window into the world of everyday consumption. Just counting the sheer number of packages we process on a weekly basis both at home and at work offers a glimpse of the scale of the issue. Multiply that number by, say, one billion, two billion, or even six billion, and you begin to understand how many packages are, or could become, tributaries to the world's total waste streams. But the "downstream" issues of collection, recycling, landfilling, and incinerating, while consequential, are dwarfed by the "upstream" consequences of packaging production. Environmental entrepreneur and author

Paul Hawken has reported that less than 2 percent of the annual waste stream is ultimately recycled—because so many impacts go unrecognized. Meanwhile, Americans transform 500 trillion pounds of resources into nonproductive solids and gases (in the form of waste water, carbon dioxide emissions, hazardous wastes, mine tailings, and construction debris, among other elements and materials) over the course of a decade.[15] Truly understanding packaging's planetary "footprint," then, is an impossibly complex task. Think of all that is necessary to transport, store, refrigerate, and distribute food and beverages. Or how many products are assembled from component parts that arrive in their own packaging from origins all over the world. For a more complete picture, we have to look upstream to the mines, forests, farms,

Simplified Packaging Chain

Upstream		Downstream
Raw Material Sourcing → Processing → Design → Manufacture → Distribution → Use → Post-Consumption		
Inputs:	**Outputs:**	**Deliverables:**
Energy	Airborne emissions	Product protection
Water	Waterborne emissions	Convenience
Raw materials	Solid waste	Theft deterrence
Labor	Habitat impacts	Storage
Transportation	Climate impacts	Information
Infrastructure	Human community impacts	Branding and marketing
		Preservation

factories, refineries, energy plants, and other places that make packaging possible.

● **Energy.** Energy production and use is probably the most significant input into all forms of packaging, as it is necessary nearly every step of the way to transform mined and harvested raw materials into finished products. In an effort to cut costs, packaging converters have relentlessly worked to decrease the amount of energy needed to produce individual packages. But even concerted efforts at energy conservation—one of the most urgent concerns of our time—face enormous challenges with increasing populations continually consuming more energy. China is powering its economic and industrial boom largely through a rapid expansion of coal-burning power plants, which emit significantly more greenhouse gases per unit of electricity than either oil or natural gas. Even exploring for new sources of energy has enormous impacts. According to a study from the National Academy of Sciences, methane released from oil and gas drilling is twice as high as previously thought.[16]

● **Paper.** According to one estimate, producing 1 ton of paper consumes over 98 tons of resources. Road-building and industrial-harvesting practices degrade ecosystems, affecting species and threatening the long-term stability of forests. Processing virgin wood fibers is an energy-, water-, and chemical-intensive process. At best, only half of those virgin wood fibers become paper. Chlorine-bleaching processes—which still dominate North American paper production—can create hazardous byproducts that are nearly impossible to detect and even harder to dispose of. An average mill using standard chlorine bleaching releases 35 tons of organochlorines daily, while lower-impact elemental chlorine-free (ECF) mills belch out 10 tons.[17] Pulp and paper is responsible for 11 percent of the total volume of water used in industrial activities throughout OECD countries.[18] On the plus side, there is a brisk, though cyclical, global trade in recycled, paperboard packaging.

● **Aluminum.** One ton of mined bauxite ore (hauled internationally from remote regions typically to areas with plentiful hydropower production) is required to produce a half ton of aluminum oxide. That, in turn, yields a quarter ton of aluminum metal. The smelting of aluminum consumes so much energy that it has earned the nickname "congealed energy." Aluminum ingots are heated, cold rolled, rolled again, transported, punched, formed, washed, painted, coated, filled, topped, boxed, palletized, and so on as they serve the ever-expanding beverage industry. Even though manufacturing aluminum from recycled materials requires 20 times (2,000 percent) less energy, post-consumer recovery rates are still lagging around the 50 percent mark in many countries. Japan and Brazil lead the world in aluminum recycling with respective recovery rates of 72 percent (1997 figures) and 61 percent (1996 figures).[19]

● **Glass.** One of our earliest industrial containers, glass is born of sand, soda ash, limestone, and cullet (recycled crushed glass), melted in furnaces to high heats of 2,700 degrees Fahrenheit. Recycling glass saves one-quarter to one-third the energy over virgin materials production. Over the decades, glass engineers have consistently optimized materials and container shapes to save weight without sacrificing strength. Since the late 1970s, glass use has been steadily replaced by plastics in the push toward single-use disposable packaging. In terms of old-fashioned local economies, refillable glass bottles have the most efficient materials-to-use ratios. Finland, which produces less packaging waste per capita than any of its European neighbors, requires that all bottled beverages produced in the country are returnable. (The average life of a returnable glass bottle is five to ten years with approximately five fillings per year).[20]

● **Steel.** Upstream in the manufacturing of a steel can, iron ore is excavated in open pit mines. A second essential ingredient, coal, is mined, a process that in the United States has increasingly involved the removal of mountain tops. Far from these activities, limestone is quarried to obtain lime for the formation of pure iron. In energy-intensive blast furnaces, iron ore is converted to pig iron, while coal is converted to coke. These two processes cause most of the pollution associated with steel production. The U.S. steel industry's air emissions rank second only to car exhaust and discharge twice as much carbon monoxide as the pulp and paper industry, the next-largest industrial source.[21] For every pound of steel, 250 pounds (31 gallons) of water is used.[22] Post-consumer steel food and beverage cans are 100 percent recyclable, although, according to the Tellus Institute, a nonprofit environmental research group, no more than 40 percent scrap is normally used in the blast oxygen furnaces where steel packaging is typically made.[23]

● **Plastic.** Plastics are one of the many products refined from crude oil, which is expected to become in increasingly limited supply within the next few decades. According to one life-cycle study, 270 million tons of oil and gas are used per year for fuels and materials stock to manufacture plastic packaging in the United States alone. In terms of recyclability, PET and polyethylene are the most commonly recycled plastic resin types, but plastics increasingly comprise comingled materials to fulfill a variety of functions. Therefore, the recyclability of plastics will probably decrease rather than expand. In addition to landscape and habitat degradation due to the drilling and transport of raw oil, the emission of particulates into the atmosphere due to plastic production and incineration raises significant questions about human and ecosystem health. Some experts say that renewable feedstocks and, most important, renewable energy hold the key to greener plastics production.

In Packages We Trust

Increasing our reliance on packaged goods makes it possible for us to export the costs and impacts of production to faraway places. It also plays the role of divider and conqueror, transforming us from loyal regions of bulk-buying citizens into a world of more than six billion individually targeted, single-portion consumers. Rather than develop relationships with familiar producers and counter clerks, we interact with packaged goods. "The central role of packaging in American culture," writes popular culture scholar Thomas Hine in *The Total Package*, "has been to replace human relationships, which are ambiguous, time-consuming, unpredictable,

and emotionally taxing, with expressive but less demanding containers."[24] Reliance on industrially produced, faraway commodities has also helped to foster a faith in the packaged commodities and a mistrust of unprocessed essentials, such as tap water and fresh foods. This spreading fear of a contaminated environment has spawned legions of buyers of bottled water, pasteurized egg and dairy products, and irradiated meats and seafood.

Packaging can be highly misleading, however, erecting a barrier between the consumer and product history that is difficult to penetrate. Single-serving water bottles emblazoned with panoramas of glaciated alpine peaks don't have to disclose that the water did not necessarily come from a mountain spring or pristine wilderness area. Or that two

De-evolution. The egg shell is Nature's timeless packaging. Molded pulp, consisting largely of recycled fibers, was a late-19th-century technology. Today most eggs are produced in large confined-animal feeding operations where hens live out their lives in cages. As a result, the eggs are now processed, pasteurized, and packaged in multilayered aseptic cartons. When circumstances permit, the cartons can be downcycled into tissue paper.

gallons of water might have been expended in the filtering process for every gallon that ended up in the seldom-recycled containers. Cheerful selling copy on coated paperboard cartons don't have to reveal that cut-up and frozen "free range" chickens could have lived their lives in near total confinement, regardless of what the colorful graphics and words suggest. *Buyer be aware.*

With the exception of purchase and consumption, we become completely divorced from the process of producing goods, from the impacts associated with raw material harvest and procurement, from those who made them and under what conditions, from the habitats affected along the way, as well as from the many intricate levels of assembly and transportation required to manufacture and distribute a final product. In his outstanding essay "The Whole Horse," Wendell Berry writes:

> To the extent that we participate in the industrial economy, we do not know the histories of our families or of our habitats or of our meals. This is an economy, and in fact a culture, of the one-night stand. . . . In this condition, we may have many commodities, but little satisfaction, little sense of the sufficiency of anything. The scarcity of satisfaction makes of our many commodities, in fact, an infinite series of commodities, the new commodities invariably promising greater satisfaction than the older ones. . . .

The global economy institutionalizes a global ignorance, in which producers and consumers cannot know or care about one another and in which the histories of all products will be lost. In such a circumstance, the degradation of products and places, producers and consumers is inevitable. . . . But in a sound local economy, in which producers and consumers are neighbors, nature will become the standard of work and production. Consumers who understand their economy will not tolerate the destruction of the local soil or ecosystem or watershed as a cost of production. Only a healthy local economy can keep nature and work together in the consciousness of the community. Only such a community can restore history to economics.[25]

Following Berry's logic, we must begin to see our purchases and their packages as part of larger economic and cultural systems. And, ideally, a package should be viewed as an inherent part of its product, rather than separate from it. That is, a biodegradable wrapper on an industrially produced fast-food item won't absolve that product's questionable human health and environmental hazards. And an overnight airmailed courier package will still be seen as a luxury with consequences to air pollution and global warming, even when it arrives in an envelope made from 100 percent recycled newsprint.

Does Packaging Waste Equal More Food?

Ever since Napoleon's army succeeded at storing food in cork-stoppered glass jars, and the English navy pioneered tinplate cans opened by hammer and chisel, one of packaging's most highly touted social contributions has been its success in reducing food waste through preservation and long-distance transport. And though packaging and food have developed side by side in industrialized nations since the early 1800s, many impoverished regions of the world remain hindered by a lack of packaging technologies and inadequate distribution systems. Without the means to process, store, and distribute crop surpluses, food resources go underutilized. In fact, analysis has shown that an inverse correlation exists between packaging waste and food waste.[26] In other words, the more packaging you generate, the more food you make available to the average household. In countries with highly centralized food-processing systems, cut-offs and inedible portions are typically discarded en masse at the plant. In the year 2000, for every 100 pounds of goods or food waste thrown away by Americans, 65 pounds of packaging waste were also thrown out.[27] Municipal waste streams in many developing countries, by contrast, contain substantially greater amounts of food scraps and less food packaging from individual households.

One study from the United Kingdom suggests that, from an energy-use standpoint, packaging accounts for a relatively minor share of the total energy expended throughout the life cycle of a modern processed food item. Nearly half of the total energy consumed goes into farming, fishing, harvesting, packing, and processing. Primary and secondary packaging, consumer transport, and distribution combine for just 18 percent of a processed food item's embodied energy. This means that far more upstream energy (and other resources) can be wasted if a package fails to properly deliver its product.[28] (Fresh, locally grown foods, however, can require less energy to produce and distribute.)

The food industry claims that, while not quite perfect, our modern food system is the safest in history. And with Americans taking one of every two meals outside the home, and even relying on pre-processed foods when "cooking" at home, packaging plays a pivotal role in the way we eat. (Microwave popcorn serves as an excellent example. We no longer even have the time to heat up oil in a pan.) Thanks to feats of modern packaging technologies, shelf lives of highly perishable meats, seafood, and produce have been greatly extended. High-acid drinks and foods can be contained. Meal preparation time is cut exponentially. However, this is food of a certain kind—food that is transported long distances, often refrigerated, highly processed, frequently irradiated, sterilized, and wrapped in lightweight plastics.

Despite these packaging breakthroughs, the actual safety and nutritional value of processed foods is often questionable. A recent study released

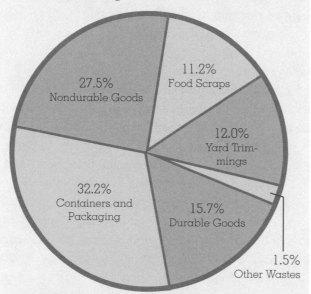

Products Generated in U.S. Municipal Solid Waste, 2000

- 11.2% Food Scraps
- 27.5% Nondurable Goods
- 12.0% Yard Trimmings
- 32.2% Containers and Packaging
- 15.7% Durable Goods
- 1.5% Other Wastes

Packaging Rules the Waste Stream. Containers and packaging represent the largest segment of U.S. municipal solid waste, with 32 percent, or 75 million tons. Residential waste is estimated at between 55 and 65 percent of total waste generation. That places commerical waste (including waste from schools, commercial enterprises, etc.) at between 35 and 45 percent of total waste generation. After a decade of steady recycling efforts, almost 39 percent of all containers and packaging were recovered for recycling in 2000. Material recovery rates were as follows: aluminum, 55 percent; steel, 58 percent; paper and paperboard (primarily corrugated cardboard), 56 percent; wood (retired pallets), 6 percent; glass, 26 percent; plastics (primarily soft drink, milk, and water bottles), 9 percent.

Source: U.S. Environmental Protection Agency, "Municipal Solid Waste in the United States: 2000 Facts and Figures," Executive Summary, 7.

by the *Journal of the American Medical Association* reported that two-thirds of adult Americans are at least 30 pounds over average weight.[29] One-third of these are considered medically obese—more than 100 pounds overweight. Writing in the *New York Times Magazine*, food and agriculture writer Michael Pollan explains that, due to the obesity crisis and the modern industrial diet, "some researchers predict that today's children will be the first generation of Americans whose life expectancy will actually be shorter than that of their parents."[30] According to Eric Schlosser, author of *Fast Food Nation*, 75 million Americans suffered from some form of food poisoning in 2001.[31]

Another irony of our age of plenty lies in the amazing disparities between the shelf life of the food items we package and the shelf life of the packages themselves. A coffee is downed in ten minutes, whereas the Styrofoam cup that contained it could outlast the marble of Michaelangelo's David. The same applies for that cream pie in an aluminum tray or any other product with a shelf expectancy of six months and a landfill expectancy of many centuries.

Food security is a growing concern in this new era of bioterrorism, but we are simultaneously waging a war against freshness in the name of keeping foods "clean and safe." Rather than moving toward a culture of health and beauty, where our nutrition is derived from fresh foods grown sustainably by local or even national farmers, we seem to be lurching toward a future of hyper-processing and ever-escalating individual portions. "Smart" packages of the future, we are told, will become more customized: containing vitamin supplements, drugs, and other additives. (Ginko, brain-enhancing, joint-relaxing snack bars, for example.) They'll also contain auto-ID tracer tags that inform manufacturers where you purchased them, when they were opened, and how they were disposed of. Time/temperature integrators will monitor whether perishable goods with a short shelf life have been stored at the proper temperatures. Smart packages embedded with computer chips will reorder themselves in our smart refrigerators connected to the Internet. "Active" packaging will let oxygen in or keep it out, heat or cool contents with a twist, give off light, emit sounds, and produce other sensations. "Everything will be connected in a dynamic, automated supply chain that joins businesses and consumers together in a mutually beneficial relationship," predicts Dr. Mary K. Schmidl, adjunct professor in the Department of Food Science and Nutrition at the University of Minnesota.[32] If all this sounds too conspiratorial or far-fetched, consider the observations of one packaging consultant who explains that one of the driving inspirations for the processed food and packaging industry is providing fresh salad for the three-year trip to Mars.[33]

Food packaging alone is roughly a $105 billion industry in the United States—of which 40 percent is paperboard (holding steady) and 20 percent is plastic (growing rapidly). This industrial food complex stands in stark contrast to the less energy-intensive, more regionally based food systems in many other parts of the world, and to the "buy local" campaigns advocated by organic farming associations, farmers markets, and community-supported agriculture producers in many countries.

Considering the broader impacts of food and packaging production, we soon have to address whether it is desirable for the rest of the world to increase its packaging 10- to 20-fold in imitating food systems of the industrialized world. In striving toward sustainable development, do we want to emphasize systems that rely on locally produced foods to feed our local regions or systems that depend on industrial commodities to feed the world? What types of processed food packaging promote positive cultural and nutritional values, and which are merely marketing driven and devious in nature? How can we develop food systems that are inclusive, nonelitist, and humane? How do international distribution and industrial harvesting and processing methods affect key local resource bases, such as fisheries, productive soils, and forests? A well-rounded "whole systems approach" is needed to evaluate the increasingly complex trade-offs and values of packaging.

Intrinsic Environmental Consequences of Trade-Related Transport

by Jerry Mander and Simon Retallack

The central feature of an export-oriented production model is that it dramatically increases transport and shipping activity. In the half-century since Bretton Woods [the agreement that established the post–World War II international monetary system], there has been about a 25-fold increase in global transport activity.

As global transport increases, it in turn requires massive increases in global infrastructure development. This is good for large corporations like Bechtel, which get to do the construction work: new airports, seaports, oil fields, pipelines for the oil, rail lines, high-speed highways. Many of these are built in areas with relatively intact wilderness, biodiversity, and coral reefs, or they

are built in rural areas. The impact is especially strong now in South and Central America, where there have been tremendous investments in infrastructure development in wilderness regions, often against great resistance from native communities like the U'wa in Columbia, the Kuna in Panama, and many different groups in Ecuador. The problems also occur in the developed world. In the United Kingdom a few years ago, there were protests by two hundred thousand people against huge new highways jammed through rural landscapes so that trucks could better serve the global trading system. Both the indigenous protesters and the rural English were protesting the same thing—the ecological destruction of their region to serve globalization.

Increased global trade increases fossil-fuel use as well, contributing to global warming. Ocean shipping carries nearly 80 percent of the world's international trade in goods. The fuel commonly used by ships is a mixture of diesel and low-quality oil known as "Bunker C," which is particularly polluting because of high levels of carbon and sulphur. If

not consumed by ships, it would otherwise be considered a waste product. The shipping industry is anticipating major growth over the next few years; the port of Los Angeles alone projects a 50 percent increase over the next decade.

Increased air transport is even more damaging than shipping. Each ton of freight moved by plane uses 49 times as much energy per kilometer as when it's moved by ship. A physicist at Boeing once described the pollution from the takeoff of a single 747 like "setting the local gas station on fire and flying it over your neighborhood." A two-minute takeoff by a 747 is equal to 2.4 million lawnmowers running for 20 minutes.

Ocean pollution from shipping has reached crisis levels, and there have been direct effects of these huge ships on wildlife and fisheries. Even more serious, possibly, is the epidemic increase of bioinvasions, a significant cause of species extinction. With the growth of global transport, billions of creatures are on the move. Invasive species, brought by global trade, often outnumber native species and bring pollution or health crises. In the United States, the emergence of the West Nile virus where it never existed before is due to increased transport activity. So is the spread of malaria and dengue fever.

Ocean shipping also requires increased refrigeration—contributing to ozone depletion and climate change—and an increase in the packaging and the wood pallets used for cargo loading; these are little-noted but significant factors in increased pressure on global forests.

Global conversion of agriculture from diverse, small-scale local farms to giant, chemical-intensive industrial production for export markets have also brought terrible environmental destruction to lands and waters across the planet.

The central point is this: if you are going to design a system built on the premise that dramatically increased global trade and transport is good, you are guaranteed to bring on these kinds of environmental problems. They are intrinsic to the model.

Excerpted, with permission, from Alternatives to Economic Globalization: A Better World Is Possible *(San Francisco: Berrett-Koehler, 2002), 28–29.*

Upstream in the Energy Flow. Energy is a major component of modern packaging, particularly in the processing of materials and in manufacturing. In addition to supplying much-needed water and electricity, large-scale internationally financed dam projects have left a legacy of ecological and social consequences.

Acceptable Levels of Waste

Just as in the United States we tolerate certain levels of water and air pollution, soil contamination, toxics accumulation, global warming, biodiversity loss—even highly toxic pesticide residues on our children's food—the global consumer society is predicated upon acceptable levels of packaging waste. (It is interesting to note that we talk about streams of waste, as if they were naturally occurring features on the landscape, and yet there is nothing resembling such degradation in a healthy ecosystem. Perhaps mountains would be the more appropriate analogy.) Waste is what remains after the trade-offs among cost reduction, product manufacture, transportation impacts, distribution hazards, material availability, and other factors are weighed, sorted, and measured. Pollution allowances are based on the premise that controlled releases will "dilute and disperse" in the air or water and so be rendered harmless.

But at the molecular level some chemicals do not simply vaporize—they can accumulate in organs and tissues, move across food webs, and come back to haunt us.[34] Dioxins are potent carcinogens that travel airborne and waterborne across local, regional, and even national boundaries. Discharged wastewater becomes an uncontained toxic fluid that moves and transforms streams, rivers, lakes, and other water bodies. By permitting such unsustainable manufacturing impacts today,

among other atrocities, we foist the clean-up bills on future generations of citizens and taxpayers, and today's waste becomes a form of deficit spending. "Ultimately a regulation is a signal of a design failure," William McDonough and Michael Braungart argue in their book *Cradle to Cradle*. "In fact it is what we call a license to harm: a permit issued by a government to an industry so that it may dispense sickness, destruction, and death at an 'acceptable' rate."[35] (This should not be interpreted as an argument for the abandonment of regulation, however, but as a signal that our laws and enforcement agencies are no longer adequately protecting us.)

Solid waste has also become a commodity with free movement between states, and there is a brisk trade in numerous kinds of recovered packaging. Today, waste collection in industrialized countries is becoming ever more mechanized with high-tech systems to collect, sort, and process municipal waste; humans are involved only as drivers and machine operators. Materials recovery facilities (MRFs, known as *murfs*) are the latest evolution in waste recovery systems, where tractors, conveyor systems, people, laser-aided material sorters, and other contraptions recycle, reuse, and compost dozens of materials and hope one day to render garbage a thing of the past. Modern glass recycling centers almost miraculously sort different colored glass pieces with high-tech lasers and blowers, discarding the odd Barbie Doll appendage or golf ball that errantly makes its way into the cullet. Meanwhile, in many developing countries, whole classes of citizens live the hazardous existence of scavenger cooperatives, picking, eating, and sorting in landfills. In Brazil, for example, a conservative estimate of 50,000 *catadores* sort open dumps largely for trade in recyclables, including aluminum cans, glass bottles, and plastic packaging materials such as PET water bottles for local processing or export to Asia. These garbage sorters are so effective that popular wisdom holds an aluminum can thrown away in Brazil never touches the ground.

Although burying more than 75 million tons of potential resources each year in the United States in the form of discarded packaging is obviously unproductive, many argue (plastic advocates in particular) that landfills serve an invaluable environmental benefit. With the exception of the Northeast, manmade crater space is considered to be plentiful in most areas of the United States (although that is slowly changing). It might be best to keep these solid waste repositories lined and sealed airtight, to prevent the leaching and off-gassing of unwanted chemicals such as bleaches, adhesives, dyes, heavy metals, and so on into soil and groundwater. Another pro-landfill argument is that the anaerobic (oxygen-free) condition of such sites can also lessen decomposition, which generates methane gas and carbon dioxide and adds to global warming.

The capitalist logic behind a landfill is understandable. Once approved, the owners, who are obviously performing a community service, have a captive clientele for the next 20 years until the dump fills up. And, there is a significant difference between a "collectable" and "recyclable" package. Some municipalities have established recycling systems, while others have not. As a result, the recovery and reprocessing of materials is not always economically or even environmentally effective. In the absence of integrated systems that unite manufacturers, reprocessors, consumers, and others, however, landfills are inevitable.

This pro-landfill reasoning stands in contrast to the increasingly popular notion of a new industrial revolution in which a high percentage of materials would reenter the materials stream by virtue of being compostable, biodegradable, or easily separable into highly reusable "technical nutrients" such as metals, resins, and other recoverable elements. By designing for disassembly and reprocessing in the first place, we can perhaps achieve a world beyond waste, where products become services that are leased rather than sold, and essential industrial materials are continually reprocessed in endless loops of materials, compost, or energy generation.

Curbside Confessionals

It is true that, in the past decade, recycling programs around the world have returned ever-increasing volumes of materials to production streams. Up to 100 million Americans, in fact, recycle every day, although overall recycling rates have begun to decline in recent years.[36] In the year 2000, the U.S. Environmental Protection Agency published a report on rates of municipal solid waste (see graph on page 20). Within West European countries, packaging waste is estimated to be approximately 17 percent of the total municipal solid-waste stream thanks to a decade of legislative and industry efforts to increase recycling.[37] In many countries, the definition of recycling has also included incineration.

But many argue that, rather than dramatically reducing our use of virgin materials, recycling can serve to justify maintaining or boosting present levels of consumption. (Because the packaging is collectable, we grow careless about our consumption habits and thereby miss an essential point: even recycling has an impact of some kind.) In addition, recovered materials are most often downcycled into inferior products, buried, or burned at least partly because very few have been specifically formulated and manufactured for recyclability in the first place. Perhaps even more important, the carrot of potential recyclability (or compressability in the landfill) has perpetuated the use of many widely used petroleum-derived chemicals of which even the smallest emissions can affect developing humans and nonhuman species.

For the average citizen, participating in a curbside recycling program serves in a way as a weekly consumer confessional of sorts—a chance to ship things out of sight and out of mind into the brave new world of reuse. We may separate packaging materials into recycling bins and faithfully carry them to the curb, hoping they will reenter the materials stream rather than become solid waste. But very few of us know with any certainty whether these post-consumer castaways are bound for the incinerator, landfill, paper mill, plastics refinery, or overseas shipping container.

Although curbside recycling programs proliferated throughout the country in the 1990s, (increasing from 500 in 1990 to 8,000 just five years later),[38] the nation's discipline and enthusiasm for sorting trash seems to be fading. And when the economy slows, recycling programs are among the first to get the hatchet. Faced with rising budget deficits, mayors in cities big and small across the United States are considering charging residents or slashing 10-year-old recycling programs in order to save green—short-term cash, that is. Perhaps most vocal has been New York City mayor Michael Bloomberg, who has said he believes recycling "does nothing to help the environment." Seattle, once a beacon of recycling, has seen its citywide waste diversion rate drop from 44 percent to 38 percent in recent years, perhaps not coincidentally during a time when working hours are increasing.[39]

Tracking a Package's Footsteps

Over the past decade, bringing to light the nitty-gritty details of a packaging material's "hidden life" has been the goal of a Pandora's box–like pursuit called "life-cycle analysis" or "life-cycle assessment" (LCA). At its best, an LCA has a noble goal: untangling the intricate flows of energy, raw materials, pollution, transportation, and other factors in the hope of accounting for all the environmental and social costs of production. But true LCAs can take years and tens of thousands of dollars to conduct—and for most decision makers, they're far too complicated. In addition, packaging is now produced and recovered globally, under vastly different sets of circumstances, technologies, and infrastructures. Although LCAs continually increase in sophistication, most experts agree that no single LCA can ever fully account for all the complex factors that make up even a single material. Almost by definition, each has its biases and limitations. Almost by default, LCAs serve only as incomplete portraits of a complete production system.

"The fundamental problem with LCAs is that the significance of environmental impacts lies in the eye of the beholder," explains Rod Miller, a long-time recycling professional and lobbyist for some of the first mandatory recycled-content legislation in the United States. "I personally think that habitat loss is more significant than landfill impacts, but what unit of habitat loss is equal to how many units of landfill or air pollution impacts? Which is more significant, habitat loss near urban areas or habitat loss in the rural rainforests? LCA is a tool for bringing out the information. It is up to all responsible citizens of the planet to decide which products have the least impact."[40]

Unfortunately, LCAs have pitted trade association against trade association, scientist against scientist, nonprofit against nonprofit, and business against business, with no clear winners or losers. LCAs have increasingly become tools of marketing departments and trade groups, and it is important that we always question the source and examine the science in any given study.

Those criticisms noted, at least a few LCAs have been conducted that help cast important light on making decisions and general assumptions about packaging materials. During the early 1990s, the Tellus Institute, based in Cambridge, Massachusetts, conducted a lengthy LCA on glass, aluminum, steel, five types of paper, and six types of plastic. According to the Tellus study, energy expenditures and emissions from collection trucks, incinerators, and other end-of-life activities often account for just 1 percent of a package's overall impact.[41] The most serious external costs of packaging lie instead in the extraction of natural resources, energy consumption, and the emission of air and water pollution throughout the manufacturing processes. "As unattractive as it is to live next to the newest, cleanest landfill," wrote Dr. Frank Ackerman, a Tufts University professor who participated in the study, "it might be 100 times as bad for your health to live next to a paper mill, oil refinery, or steel mill."[42] Another LCA was conducted in the mid-1990s by Environmental Defense/Alliance for Environmental Innovation and a mainstream coalition of corporate and educational partners, in an effort to make recommendations for purchasing and using "environmentally preferable" papers. Most environmentalists agreed that the 250-page report of data collection provided a valuable service by deconstructing the environmental impacts of massive-scale paper production.[43] Some of the findings showed that paper is the most capital- and water-intensive industry, that it ranks third in hazardous effluent due to the pulping and bleaching processes, and that it ranks fourth in terms of energy consumption.

Some general rules of thumb have emerged: (1) Manufacturing with recycled materials almost always uses less water and energy, and it results in less-toxic byproducts than working with virgin materials, so priorities should be given for resource optimization. (2) Truly chlorine-free bleaching technologies for papermaking are superior in nearly every way compared to chlorine-based manufacturing techniques. And (3) the classic 3R formula—reduce (eliminate), reuse (refill), and recycle (reprocess)—holds up well to close scrutiny.

Yet understanding even a single, narrow factor within an LCA requires a multidisciplinary approach. Take, for example, rough averages for energy consumption of the four primary means of product transportation, based on data supplied by the Department of Energy:[44]

Energy Consumption Related to Transport				
Mode	Rail	Boat	Truck	Plane
Btus/ton-mile	371	411	4,359	31,609
Energy Factor	1	1	12	85

On the surface, says Mike Brown, an environmental consultant based in Santa Barbara, California, who helped reform Patagonia's production practices throughout the 1990s, it seems that boat transportation is one of our most preferred choices, because of its relatively low energy consumption.[45] But other critical environmental impacts come into play: a boat's total emissions into the air and ocean, or the unintended transfer of exotic invasive species (through bilge water, for example), with the potential to devastate ecosystems.

Perhaps the real value of such studies lies not in black-and-white answers but in identifying the important trade-offs involved in making packaging decisions, and in setting priorities for future work. Carl Rabago, former sustainability alliances leader for Cargill Dow, a corn-based plastics manufacturer, explains that LCAs can be used strategically to set improvement priorities as well as to analyze and monitor results over a given time period.[46]

In order to make critical choices about packaging options, the narrow materials assessments of

LCAs are probably best combined with broader assessments of how compatible a particular product and package fits into economic and social systems. Such an integrated "whole systems" approach would attempt to place packaging impacts in a more complete light, including (but not limited to) the life cycle of the package itself; the manufacturing and distribution system in which it functions; the geographic and political arenas in which it circulates; and, perhaps most important, the actual product that it packages. For example, PET plastic might be the most appropriate material in which to ship filtered water from France to California because of its light weight and potential recyclability. But is it an appropriate use of resources to ship single servings of filtered water across the ocean? The package is no longer a plastic vessel but an integral part of the product: imported drinking water and all that embodies.

Energy Required to Make Packaging Materials (Btus per gram of material)	
Recycled Glass	6
Recycled Unbleached Paperboard	7
Virgin Glass	8
Recycled Aluminum	10
Recycled HDPE	12
Virgin Unbleached Paperboard	22
Virgin HDPE	88
Virgin Aluminum	182

Source: "Relative Production Energy Chart," Alliance for Environmental Innovation, 2001.

In Search of Water from a Deeper Well

The issue of bottled water brings up an interesting window into the world of modern packaging. In just a few short decades, the bottled-water industry has emerged as a beverage powerhouse, competing with soft drinks and health drinks for consumer dollars. According to Maude Barlow and Tony Clarke, authors of *Blue Gold: The Fight to Stop the Corporate Theft of the World's Water*, the quantity of bottled water traded worldwide has been doubling each decade since the 1970s. By the turn of the new century, for example, 22.3 billion U.S. gallons (some 84 billion liters) were bottled and sold, up from just 300 million gallons in 1970.[47] The bottle toll adds up to 1.5 million tons of plastics per year. In California alone, 1.2 billion single-serving water bottles are discarded annually, enough material to fill San Francisco's baseball stadium 70 feet deep.[48]

One has to wonder why this rapid social transformation toward single-use water containers has come about. A simple answer is that the bottled water industry has merely served the pent-up demands of our on-the-go and ever-safety-conscious society. Never matter that the product can cost more than wine, milk, or petroleum.

Plunging beneath the surface of the bottled-water phenomenon, however, yields some startling findings. Twenty-five percent of bottled water is traded and consumed outside its country of origin.[49] Moreover, another 25 percent is actually tap water,

which, in some countries, is subject to questionable regulatory standards and scrutiny. Investigative studies have also brought the purity of bottled waters into question. A 1999 study by the Natural Resources Defense Council, for example, found that 33 percent of brands sampled contained contaminants, including arsenic and *E. coli*.[50]

What of the bottle itself? Could the production of plastic and its global transport help to set the cycle of bottled water in motion? In other words, to the extent that industrial plastics manufacturing contributes to contaminated water supplies, this triggers the need for clean water sources, which requires plastic bottles that, even when recycled, generate still more energy and pollutants, making purified water even more scarce.

Some activists are calling for mandatory post-consumer-content laws that would require producers to use a given percentage of recycled materials in their bottles. Mandatory regulations would then build markets and infrastructure for collection and processing as it previously has in the glass and aluminum industries. But it must be noted that, though generally preferable to virgin production, recycling is still an energy- and water-intensive process with impacts of its own. Shifting toward recycling would also require a major shift in subsidies. According to Allen Hershkowitz, author of *Bronx Ecology*, the World Bank directed subsidies in excess of $21 billion between 1992 and 2002 for the extraction, transportation, and processing of fossil fuels, the raw materials of plastics. This is one reason, he asserts, why 96 percent of all plastics are discarded in the United States.[51]

What is perhaps most troubling about the global trade in water lies in a fundamental assault on local autonomy and ecosystems. Many parts of the world have actually sold their water rights to multinational corporations. Agricultural lands have been purchased and then later abandoned after the aquifers have been sucked dry for bottled-water operations. Wilderness areas in Latin America are being purchased for future water exploitation. Canada has become a major exporter of water to the world in the past decade; corporations there have secured the rights to extract more than 250 gallons (1,000 liters) per year for every person in the country.[52]

The mounting single-serving-bottled-water conundrum has at least one rather elegant and profound solution: clean water, flowing from taps, water coolers, fountains, and home filtration equipment, and toted around in reusable containers. That would, however, require us to develop a collective conscience and become less reliant on single-serving containers that promise convenience, quality, and security but fail to disclose or even begin to account for all of the impacts throughout the product and package's life cycle. Maude Barlow, an expert on global water issues, has said: "It is mass insanity to put this enormous amount of water in plastic bottles as we allow our public resources to decline."[53]

A World of "Less Bad" Solutions?

One of the great hazards of focusing on incremental change (what some critics call "eco-efficiency" or "environmentally preferable" alternatives) is that we box ourselves into a world of lesser evils. When it comes to modern packaging, we seem to be stuck in an endless loop of tough choices between wood and oil. While choosing the "less bad" alternative is certainly preferable to looking only after bottom-line business concerns, it merely postpones the real price we pay for cumulative degradation—deforestation, resource depletion, water contamination, habitat destruction, toxic pollution, climate change—to some future day of reckoning. The proper answer to the paper/plastic conundrum is still, "neither." Eliminate, reduce, refill, and recycle as much as possible. But, even better, develop whole new ways (or reintroduce old ones) of consuming, producing, distributing, packaging, reusing, and reprocessing products and materials that actually address the complex situations we face in this new century.

The realities of packaging reform are somewhat disconcerting, however. In poll after poll, consumers normally volunteer that they want more, not less, environmental protection, even as it applies to packaging. Nevertheless, at home, on the go, or in the marketplace, they often opt for what is more affordable, convenient, or appealingly packaged. Packaging professionals find themselves in a simi-

lar bind. Most are aware of the impacts of their profession on the environment and support voluntary efforts to minimize or eliminate them. But a recent survey by *Packaging World Magazine* reported that there is "an awkward disconnect between what packaging people want as individuals versus what their employers require for their businesses to run smoothly."[54] If it costs even fractionally more or requires significant time to start up, innovation is often quashed by the powers that be.

Consider the case of Alfred Heineken. The story goes that, while Heineken was vacationing on the Dutch Antilles Caribbean island of Curaçao in 1960, he was grief-stricken at the sight of his own company's beer bottles washing up as litter on the beach. In contrast to the closed-loop, refillable glass bottling system that recycled a single container dozens of times in his native Holland, these were one-way export vessels, discarded immediately after consumption. (Today, the ten largest breweries in the world produce 100 billion throwaway bottles per year.)[55]

Heineken responded with a futuristic container design eventually patented as the *WOBO*, short for "world bottle." In an attempt to elevate the ordinary to something extraordinary, the WOBO took aim at both form and function of the bottle. If the bottle metamorphosed into some longer-lived object, such as a building material, Heineken reasoned, its time as a container would merely be temporary. Rather than a short happy life, it would live on with some loftier purpose. After significant trial and error, the Heineken design team succeeded in transforming the everyday beer bottle into a glass brick that could be laid on its side, interlocked, and embedded in mortar. To test this somewhat radical notion, two opposing sides of the bottle were flattened, leaving the other two sides rounded for strength. In addition, the bottle's bottom had a recessed cavity to slip snugly into the neck of the bottle beside it.

According to authors Edward Denison and Guang Yu Ren, "despite manufacturing 50,000 of the two sizes of green-tinted Heineken WOBO bottles in 1963 and the filing of patent applications worldwide, Alfred Heineken's design became so beset with problems presented to it from outside the realm of functional design, it became unworkably compromised. As a familiar and worrying example for those wishing to instigate positive change, Heineken, so disheartened by the recurrent obstacles aimed at his WOBO, was forced to abandon the project."[56] It is difficult to say whether the WOBO's demise was strictly due to excessive costs, lack of market acceptance, or even design imperfections. Yet not even a motivated, influential, corporate leader was able to mitigate the impacts of the packaging of international beverage production through a design innovation.

The same holds true for companies that depend on wholesalers for the distribution of their goods. Many mass-market retailers, for instance, demand that products be packaged in "blister packs," the clear, rigid, plastic, planklike material that is tough to cut through and therefore theft-resistant. These clear packs also hold vast marketing potential and are often billboarded many times the size of the original product. This is known among frustrated manufacturers as "the Wal-Mart or Costco factor." These clear packs can be made from PVC, one of the most toxic of our plastics, which generates dioxins in both the manufacturing and the incineration stages. While many companies and their designers consider these packages odious, their retail distributors demand them, erecting a serious barrier to change.

The WOBO. The World Bottle or "WOBO," spearheaded by Alfred Heineken in the 1960s, was an attempt to give glass bottles an extended life as bricks. Two sides of the containers were flattened and bottles could be interlocked through a recessed cavity in the bottom. While ingeniously conceived to facilitate construction of glass walls, the WOBO failed to gain industry acceptance.

Can Packaging Have a Meaningful Life?

It is amazing how an ordinary commodity like packaging allows us to plumb an existential question, one that cuts to the heart of the human condition—*Why are we here?* What will garbologists rummaging through landfills millennia from now glean from the still-legible labels compressed in veins of discarded packaging hermetically sealed below the surface of the earth? Certainly packages make our lives easier. They provide value, convenience, consistency, and an undeniable sense of self-sufficiency. They bring us fruits and vegetables, shoes and socks, crayons and paints, medicine and libations, books and music, duct tape and plastic buckets, sunscreen and dental floss. They take the place of dealing with other humans—their moods and shortcomings. Packages keep our economies running by feeding the machines of efficiency calibrated by the millions of "stock-keeping units." Certainly the negative impacts of the individual packages we consume pale in comparison to other environmental woes, such as the proliferation of gas-guzzling automobiles, the pollution from energy plants, and habitat destruction related to all kinds of resource extraction and development to support an ever-increasing human population. But

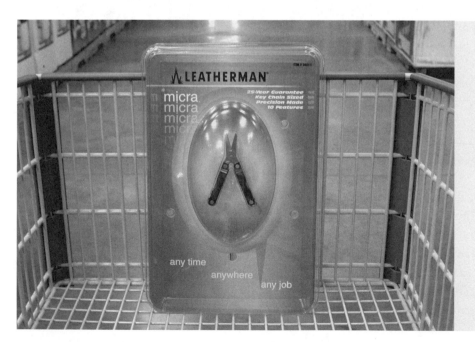

Consumer Conundrum. Many retail chains require manufacturers to wrap products in clamshell blister packs for theft prevention as well as marketing. This package is about eight times the size of the product it packages. Ironically, you need a tool like the one contained to open this pack.

those impacts cannot be separated from our overall relation to the earth and its many ecosystems.

If we really want to change our relationship with packaging—a relationship that helps us keep the realities of production and delivery at arm's length—then we must certainly look beyond the paper versus plastic argument. We must first be willing to envision how products and their packages fit into broader economic, political, environmental, and social systems—that is, determine whether these economic systems move us toward ecological and social harmony or away from it. Rather than settle for the status quo of lesser evils, we may need to reorder our priorities and change how we live our lives, most likely on a massive scale.

Ideally, after packaging has served its initial purpose, it should be returned for reuse or remanufacture, or it should fulfill a compostable or edible function. No product, however flawed, should be redeemed by a "green" package and vice versa. No product, however green, should arrive in an unacceptable wrap. Consumer awareness at its best would actively minimize consumption (including packaging) and support, as much as possible, products of quality, durability, and local or regional origins.

Seriously pursuing the ideal of sustainable development will require nothing less than a cultural movement, a shifting outside the realm of acceptable levels and tolerable risks. Just as reversing climate change and global warming will require drastic advances in conservation and mov-

ing beyond dependence on the hydrocarbon economy, so halting the attack on the world's biodiversity will require an end to ecosystem-destroying material-procurement methods and an end to dependence on toxic materials that are transported freely around the planet. Lurking below the surface of all serious discussions of sustainability is the issue of human population growth and ever-increasing affluence. According to Arne Naess, one of Europe's leading 20th-century philosophers, "Every week counts. How terrible and shamefully bad conditions will be in the 21st century, or how far down we fall before we start on the way back up, depends upon what YOU and others do today and tomorrow. There is not a single day to be lost. We need activism on a high level immediately."[57]

Is it possible, when all transgressions and benefits and destiny are tallied, that packaging has served some greater purpose, or is it merely the price of convenience in a consumer culture unconcerned about its legacy? When we are confronted with unacceptable packaging, it would be nice if we were able to identify the culpable person or entity along the packaging chain: the designer, manufacturer, forester, government agent, industry lobbyist, consumer. But in fact packaging lives within systems and subsystems for which we are all somehow culpable. Our challenge is to bring these issues and occasional paradoxes to light and, in the process, educate ourselves about the consequences of manufacturing and consumption.

Instead of taking the path of least resistance, comb supermarket aisles for bulk-purchasing opportunities.

THE SEARCH

Initiatives to reform packaging emerged from numerous sectors and with varying degrees of success in the early 1990s. European governments passed revolutionary legislation aimed at putting the onus of resource recovery and waste minimization on manufacturers and the private sector. Some companies responded by cutting material weights, maximizing post-consumer content, and eliminating packaging at the source. Design gurus began depicting a vision of a 21st-century industrial paradigm based on natural capital, biomimicry, and accounting procedures that address the long-term social and environmental consequences as well as the economic costs of doing business. Third-party certification organizations raised standards for ecologically sound and socially just business practices by uniting producers and consumers in the marketplace. Highly efficient, regionally based "mini-mills" were specifically conceived to close local resource, water, and energy loops. Scientists and manufacturers worked to make plastics from plants rather than petroleum. Activists escalated their fight to put the brakes on global deforestation and to embrace "zero waste" as an achievable and desirable long-term

Buying products of all kinds from bulk bins reduces packaging, saving energy and materials. It typically saves money, too.

FOR SOLUTIONS

strategy for communities. Citizens around the world embraced the organic and Slow Food movements, among others, in efforts to strengthen local economies.

More than a decade after the 1992 Rio Earth Summit, however, change appears to be frustratingly slow. In "mature" industries—where the infrastructure in place is massive in scale and entrenched, where profit margins are fractional and R&D hardly a consideration let alone a priority, where resource extraction is heavily subsidized—progress tends to be incremental rather than profound. By the end of the 1990s, public interest in recycling was waning, and with each passing year the pressures of population growth and economic development intensified. Still, people have tried to forge paths toward "sustainability," and the world of packaging offers the opportunity to peer into unexpected windows for signs of hope. There will be no silver bullet to solve packaging's environmental challenges. Instead, we must be open to a variety of alternatives from a diversity of perspectives, approaches, and places along the supply chain. This section provides an overview of attempts to reduce, optimize, and reform packaging.

Major Obstacles Preventing Packaging Reform

As much as we all might like to see an immediate shift to more benign packaging, there are numerous barriers to deep changes. First and foremost among these is an ever-growing number of people consuming increasing amounts of resources—including packaged commodities. Outlining the most significant obstacles can serve not only to put packaging challenges into a broader perspective but also as a way to set priorities for urgent action.

Lack of corporate leadership. With rare exceptions, corporate leaders pay lip service to environmental issues, acting only when it positively influences the economic bottom line. Profound reforms require top-level commitments that are translated throughout all areas of an organization, including energy conservation policies, phase-outs of hazardous substances and materials from endangered habitats, packaging design briefs, and so on. While most packaging professionals personally support environmental packaging initiatives, few companies truly support them.[58]

Design priorities driven by marketing and branding (rather than by environmental stewardship). Marketing departments demand ever-changing, sales-oriented designs and are often the lead decision makers in specifying packages that use more rather than fewer materials, including multilayered packs that are nonrecyclable. These hyped-up packages often sell well—so well, in fact, that they incite an escalation of packaging among competitors.

Legalized pollution tolerances. Corporations have been producing mass quantities of toxic pollution, carcinogens, and other "bad actors" for over a century, with relatively minor penalties. This has been formally legalized through the regulation of "acceptable tolerances" of poisons and carcinogens such as pesticides on farms, dioxins from the wood-bleaching process, pollutants from plastic and chemical manufacturing and incineration, nitrogen and sulfur oxides from energy production, chlorinated compounds and heavy metals in inks, dyes, and plasticizers, and so on. Many of these substances bioaccumulate in human tissue and that of other species. Many scientists fear that the Earth's ability to continually absorb toxins and excess carbon is rapidly diminishing. In addition, regulatory agencies have been infiltrated by industry in an attempt to roll back decades of legal checks on toxic releases.

Absence of distributor responsibility. This is sometimes referred to by manufacturing insiders as "the Wal-Mart or Costco factor." Large resellers and retailers require that manufacturers overpackage goods so that they can be "billboarded" and merchandised in the shelf-competitive marketplace. If manufacturers want to make the sales in these massive distribution centers, they are obliged to comply. This can mean using a large amount of a dreadful material such as PVC blister packing to encapsulate a tiny product—and the ultimate consumer risks getting cut when tearing into the rigid plastic.

●Need for integrated infrastructure developments. The lack of collaboration among competitors and within industries that could create economies of scale and promote viable alternative materials and distribution systems greatly hinders packaging reform. When developing environmentally preferable alternatives, corporations often adopt a confidential proprietary stance rather than working publicly for change. Integrated approaches that create material pools, optimize nearby resources (particularly post-consumer and post-industrial materials), and make deep connections among suppliers, converters, manufacturers, consumers, collection agencies, and so on are essential.

●Material disconnect. The dichotomy between the shelf life of a product and its packaging is often absurd. For instance, a take-out cup of coffee, usually consumed in minutes, is sometimes cupped in polystyrene foam, a material that can persist for centuries in a landfill. Furthermore, most packaging materials are not intentionally designed for recycling, which limits how and whether they can be transformed into future products.

●Need for energy conservation. Among a package's most significant environmental impacts is the energy consumed during its manufacture. Transportation and incineration are other important energy-related issues linked to packaging. Climate change is widely accepted by most objective scientists and countries as a real and urgent global threat. In order to address this crisis, the world needs to quickly develop new standards of energy efficiency, new forms of renewable energy, new methods to retrofit existing power plants and vehicles, and new strategies to sequester rather than release carbon into the atmosphere.

●Lack of worldwide and intra-industry standardization. The refusal of Americans to adopt the metric system prevents us from being a world united through standard measures that facilitate interchangeable and reusable packaging systems. Standardization among industries, such as bottle users or produce shippers, could lead to far higher rates of package reconditioning and recovery. Ironically, standardization carries its own sets of drawbacks, such as increasing the long-distance trade of basic commodities.

●Limits to recycling under current conditions. After 10 years of concerted efforts to establish state- and nationwide collection goals and to develop regional recycling and curbside collection systems, recycling rates are again declining. Some analysts say the low-hanging fruits of collection and recycling have been picked, and advancing beyond that will require far more energy, investment, and resources. Low landfill disposal fees, combined with long distances between recycling plants and dumps, keep collection costs high in many areas of the United States. Packaging recovery in the United States still lags behind Europe— 38 percent compared to the EU member states' 1998 recycling rates, which ranged from 28 percent in Italy and the United Kingdom to 65 percent in Germany.[59]

●**Consumerism and citizen apathy.** Accelerating high-speed lifestyles that value convenience, inexpensiveness, eating outside the home, and high levels of consumption undercut other important concerns, such as nutrition, environmental protection, and genuine sustainability. Some critics argue that one effect of curbside programs is to encourage consumers to buy more. Because packaging is collectable, the reasoning follows, some consumers feel justified in increasing their consumption habits.

●**Growth of industrialization and affluence.** By 2050, the human population could reach as high as 10 billion people, with dozens of additional nations joining the excess consumption party. Unprecedented population growth in the billions, combined with unprecedented economic and energy growth, will make packaging reduction extremely difficult.

●**Global capitalism.** The present global capitalist system perpetuates a number of predatory conditions: (1) the relentless movement of production to areas with cheaper labor forces and lax environmental laws or enforcement; (2) the accumulation of gigantic pools of capital in pursuit of continuous growth regardless of social or ecological costs; (3) the commodification of complex ecosystems as resources; (4) a tendency toward consolidations and cartels and away from diverse regional economies that can truly engage in "fair trade"; (5) the ability of corporations to overturn local or national environmental laws on the basis that they are anticompetitive and therefore erect unfair barriers to trade. (One packaging example: a multinational corporation successfully challenging a country's mandatory refill container laws through a government trade representative in the World Trade Organization or European Union, who argues that such laws are anticompetitive.)[60]

●**Subsidies.** Throughout the world, government subsidies facilitate the extraction of virgin materials (forest products, agricultural crops, mined metals, petroleum, and gas), thereby thwarting the development of economically competitive regional or local resource loops. These include massive supports for road building and maintenance, tax incentives for polluters, below-cost public land leasing and stumpage fees, below-market timber prices in state-owned forests, government-funded cleanups in communities where manufacturing takes place,

Paper or Plastic

and agricultural commodity crop subsidies. Consider also subsidized bulk mail rates that allow unsolicited advertising—such as one company's insidious and excessively packaged online software—to be cheaply shipped in massive quanities.

● **Bioterrorism, bioinvasion, and disease.** The Bioterrorism Law of the U.S. Homeland Security Act of 2003 will cause an exponential rise in paperwork and perhaps packaging in an effort to monitor the global food chain. The transfer of exotic pests through trade, such as the Asian longhorned beetle that has become widely infested via wood pallets, is affecting the health of hardwood forests in many regions. This has inspired new regulations requiring that all wooden transport containers engaged in international trade be made of heat-treated or chemically treated wood (often with arsenic), to be fumigated (with pesticides), or derived from alternative materials such as plastics or particle board.

● **Fear of litigation hindering refill programs.** Many U.S. corporations avoid developing container reconditioning programs for fear of being sued for someone else's subsequent reuse or misuse of a container.

● **The global waste trade.** Waste is a global commodity, which allows communities, states, and countries to export their garbage far beyond their borders. Some countries even export plastics in order to comply with their own waste diversion requirements. This allows us to live beyond the abilities of our own local ecosystems to absorb and process wastes, while turning other communities into waste colonies.

● **The crisis of obesity.** Obesity has been moving like a wave across America and other countries and has had a ripple effect throughout the entire packaging chain. Businesses have capitalized on the crisis by catering to overweight audiences with "super" sizes of foods and beverages, larger clothing sizes, retrofits of chairs in theaters and stadiums, and so on. This in turn has required more surface area of materials to package, including the ultimate end-of-life box, the oversized casket.

● **Mature industries' resistance to change.** Commodity suppliers lag far behind specifiers and designers who want to "green" the packaging chain. A lack of R&D in manufacturing industries, such as paper, is endemic. One career paper industry professional bemoaned the astounding lack of change by saying: "I became a mill manager in 1970, and I can still start up any paper machine in our company or run any winder. Isn't that tragic? I shouldn't be able to understand how it works, much less how to run it."[61]

Key Leverage Points and Trends Toward Packaging Reform

Change, as an old adage goes, is the only constant. Numerous convergent forces are making environmental issues among humanity's most critical concerns in the century ahead, and they will no doubt alter life as we know it. Packaging—a fundamental part of daily life and an increasing scourge on the landscape—will not escape these changes. The key question many experts are asking is whether change can take place rapidly enough to keep pace with the looming challenges in our path.

● **Growing markets of conscientious consumers.** Studies throughout the world show increasing audiences of consumers concerned about the environmental consequences of goods production and packaging. Motivated groups such as LOHAS (lifestyles of health and sustainability), Greens, organic and Slow Food aficionados, and environmentally concerned parents want to support companies that care about the impacts of their packaging.

● **Landfills becoming scarcer.** In 1975 the United States had 18,000 landfills; by 2000, there were just 2,300.[62] These remaining "superdumps" are repositories for faraway garbage. Approving new landfill or incinerator sites is becoming increasingly unpopular in communities all over the world.

● **Extended producer responsibility.** Begun in Germany in 1991 and considered radical in its time, extended producer responsibility (EPR) laws mandate that a package's or product's end-of-life (post-consumer life cycle) is the responsibility of its manufacturer or distributor. As of late 2003, 31 countries had adopted or were considering EPR packaging laws, meaning that manufacturers throughout the world are forced to comply with ever-stricter packaging standards if they want to continue trading in some of the largest markets. Product "take back" laws are now being extended to longer-term purchases such as computers, cell phones, batteries, tires, and cars. The United States will probably one day have to embrace EPR for packaging and other products—if not from external pressure, then out of the need to make waste management the fiscal responsibility of the private sector.

● **Empty-space laws.** These mandates determine the legal ratio of product to empty space within a container. Japan has led the way with empty-space requirements for over-the-counter drugs. South Korea imposes empty-space requirements as well as limits on layered plastic packaging materials that prevent separation and recycling.

● **Recycled content mandates.** Establishing minimum post-consumer content requirements for certain materials, such as newspapers, is an effective tool for building recycling industries. California is attempting to enforce a minimum recycled content for rigid plastic containers. Coca-Cola has apparently set a corporate-wide goal of 10 percent post-consumer content in 100 percent of its packaging.

●**The carbon-credits economy.** As the implications of global warming become more generally accepted, establishing a carbon-credits economy that would roll back energy and carbon dioxide emissions below 1990 levels is critical. Because energy is one of packaging's primary environmental impacts, carbon credits could spawn a century of enhanced conservation, renewable energy development, and incentives for sequestering carbon. As one of the world's most profligate energy users, the United States must sign on to the Kyoto Protocol and then assume a leadership role in moving beyond its standards.

●**Strengthened regional economies.** In response to the increasing globalization and unification of economies, there is a simultaneous trend toward strengthened regional and local economies. This could reduce the distances that certain types of goods are distributed, recovered, and reprocessed. Materials exchanges link local businesses with recyclers that can reuse or reprocess wastes and byproducts. Local economy advocates are attempting to link large institutional buyers with regional producers. Other types of material and resource pooling could further help establish conservation-based economies. Such regional economic growth can intensify even as trade expands.

●**Inevitable changes in available resources and other environmental factors.** Greater temperature fluctuations, increasingly unpredictable storm events, outbreaks of virulent infections, increasing costs of fossil fuels, and other environmental and societal trends are inevitable in the next few decades. These will directly or indirectly affect packaging by raising demands for materials, inducing raw-material scarcities, raising energy and transportation costs, spawning fears of the spread of deadly viruses and infections, and so on.

●**Efficiencies of scale.** As more is accomplished to reform packaging, expanding numbers of products and services increase capitalization, which in turn builds markets and magnifies the potential for deeper solutions. In some countries and economies, this is done with government participation. Europe, Japan, and U.S. states such as California are leading the way.

●**International treaties.** The Kyoto Protocol could have an important baseline effect on global energy-emissions reduction. The world's ability to forge international treaties that encourage true ecological conservation is paramount to the development of 21st-century economies.

●**Natural systems design frameworks.** Decades of merging ecology and design (i.e., "design for environment") have evolved whole new ways of looking at the entire life cycle of a product in order to make it environmentally sound, fundamentally useful, and durable, and to make its manufacture socially just. This new generation of interdisciplinary "natural systems designs" practitioners use materials and systems evaluations, life-cycle analysis, proactive consumer approaches, and other tools to address social and environmental costs during the product design process. As a result, packaging of the future may one day be derived from renewable energy, take inspiration from nature's design wisdom, and use only materials and substances that are non-toxic, biodegradable, or easily recoverable.

Landfill bans on classes of waste materials. Countries, states, and individual communities have had increasing success in banning certain types of packaging materials from landfills, such as corrugated cardboard and organic wastes, thus promoting and mandating reuse and recovery.

Tax disincentives. Taxes on nondegradable plastic shopping bags and one-way containers are controversial but could have a huge impact on the reuse and design of all kinds of materials.

Specific packaging for e-commerce. The on-demand nature of e-commerce could lend itself to a net decrease in packaging materials and increased efficiencies in transportation, although this is very difficult to quantify and hasn't yet been adequately studied. Benefits can be gained when companies adopt separate minimal packaging for e-commerce goods compared with larger, shelf-competitive retail packages. Or, as in the case of downloadable music, software, and other products, packaging can be eliminated altogether.

Moratoriums on certain packaging materials. Early bans of packaging categories focused on plastic six-pack rings, detachable beverage can tabs, ozone-depleting blowing agents in Styrofoam, and aerosol sprays. Denmark and South Korea have banned PVC packaging, and Korea has also placed a ban on expanded polystyrene foam shock-absorbing packaging. Faced with escalating consumption of disposable plastic packaging, Taiwan has taken steps to outlaw plastic shopping bags as well as disposable food packaging and tableware. Certain Chinese cities are following suit. A select number of corporations, such as Aveda and its parent company, Esteé Lauder, have taken voluntary pledges not to use PVC. An increasing number of countries are imposing bans on untreated wooden pallets to prevent the spread of deadly plant infestations. Unfortunately, this may have the effect of increasing the amount of toxic substances used to chemically treat pallets.

The Precautionary Principle. This science-based public policy tool maintains that chemicals or new technologies (including genetically modified crops and organisms) should not be approved for the market until they have been proven safe. This turns on its head the general approach to regulation in the United States, which has allowed numerous chemicals and crops to be disseminated and broadly applied wthout adequate testing. An increasing number of cities are adopting the Precautionary Principle, and it has gained popular acceptance throughout Europe. This could affect packaging through the rigorous scrutiny of future untested packaging materials.

●**Retailer responsibility.** Retailers must be held responsible for the packaging systems they require and should be considered liable for one-way and excess packaging. When Germany's Green Dot system was first introduced in 1991, it held retailers responsible for the disposal of secondary packaging if alternative collection systems were not established. Faced with receiving tons of packaging returned by customers at their checkout counters, retailers made sure an alternative system was set up by manufacturers.

●**Campaigns against corporations or industries.** Environmental groups have successfully waged targeted boycotts to protest a given company's use of a particular material or purchase of products from an endangered bioregion. Look for some of these campaigns to pursue certain types of packaging materials in the future.

●**Life-cycle analysis.** A life-cycle analysis or assessment (LCA) is one of many tools designers and others can turn to for learning about the impacts of a certain packaging system throughout its life cycle. There are now numerous desktop-computer-ready LCA software programs that are uniquely tailored for packaging designers and decision makers. Among these are Merge, IDSA Eco Indicators, BOOTS, Ugly Points, BUWAL 250, TEAM, and Eco Pro. There are also a number of general and specific studies, such as those by the Tellus Institute, the University of Michigan's Center for Sustainable Systems, and the Environmental Defense/ Alliance for Environmental Innovation, that can help in assessing impacts.

●**Packaging reform coalitions.** Initiatives are emerging in many parts of the world to bring together various stakeholders to address the "packaging problem." For example, the Sustainable Packaging Coalition was formed in 2003 by the Charlottesville, Virginia–based nonprofit, Green-Blue. O2 Global Network is an international design organization with active chapters in many leading cities and design centers. Wood-reduction activist groups are assembling constituencies to initiate reforms in the forest products industries. Ecolabel organizations, such as the Forest Stewardship Council and Chlorine-Free Products Association, are attempting to unite exemplary producers and consumers through environmental certification standards. Businesses for Social Responsibility, the Rocky Mountain Institute, and the Bioneers also work for positive change within industries.

Extended Producer Responsibility and Product Take-Back Laws

By far, the world's most draconian measures to thwart the solid waste crisis were initiated in Germany, a densely populated and industrialized country with the world's most politically influential Green Party. In 1991, faced with exporting its mounting solid waste to neighboring countries, the German government passed the "Ordinance on the Avoidance of Packaging Waste." Otherwise known as the "packaging ordinance" (*Verpackungsverordnung*), this revolutionary legislation was intended to shift the burden of packaging disposal from the public sector to the private industry producers that generate it. This was the world's first extended producer responsibility (EPR) law, attempting to hold producers and manufacturers financially accountable for the post-consumer phase of their products—specifically, for take back, recycling, and disposal of packaging. The reasoning was simple but powerful. Requiring producers to pay for their packaging's end-of-life waste management would dictate an economic imperative to become less wasteful in the first place and create a positive feedback loop for the manufacture of more economically recyclable products.

The packaging ordinance set ambitious country-wide waste recovery targets from the onset: 64 to 72 percent for various packaging materials, and a refill rate of 72 percent or higher for beverage containers. Implementing such sweeping reforms, however, posed significant short-term obstacles. Almost overnight, German consumers were encouraged to return any excessive or secondary packaging at the point-of-sale. (This change was highly unpopular with retailers.) Meanwhile, establishing the necessary infrastructure and administrative capacity to manage such a radical overhaul of the waste recovery system was complicated and costly. German industry eventually developed a two-pronged solution to the challenge, known as the Duales System Deutschland (DSD), which established a nonprofit company to collect fees by licensing a logo (*Der Grüne Punkt*, or the Green Dot) and a for-profit division to collect, separate, recycle, and process the waste.

The Green Dot symbol—a circle containing dual arrows of light and dark shades of green—quickly became the identifying mark of a new packaging era. It was not a recycling symbol but a financial one. Printed on all products for which manufacturers had paid the advance recycling fees, it alerted householders that they could place those items in curbside collection bins.

According to Bette Fishbein, a leading environmental policy analyst at the New York–based nonprofit think tank INFORM, the impacts were swift: packaging consumption decreased somewhat, packages were made lighter ("lightweighted"), unessential packaging was eliminated, the use of refill and concentrate packs increased, and shifts were made from some difficult-to-recycle composites and plastics (particularly PVC) to more easily recycled materials. In the short term, however, the government was forced to dole out nearly $30 per person per year to subsidize the unanticipated costs of implementing the program. German Greens, in the meantime, remained unsatisfied and continued to demand even more radical reforms, including bans on all plastic packaging and mandates for refillable-only beverage containers. Despite these growing pains and financial costs, this pioneering EPR legislation achieved its intended objective. Between 1991 and 1995, overall packaging decreased by 7 percent in Germany, whereas data from the U.S. Environmental Protection Agency showed a 13 percent rise in U.S. packaging consumption over the same period.[63]

1994: The European Union Follows Suit

Although Germany acted first, such changes had in fact been brewing since the oil crisis of the late 1970s and in response to various regional conditions on the continent. For better or worse, the European Union (EU) followed the 1991 German law by issuing its own "Packaging and Packaging Waste Directive" just three years later. Despite criticisms that Germany's packaging ordinance was overly bureaucratic, too myopically focused on the relatively small household waste stream, and had potentially erected unfair barriers to trade, this inter-European directive was eventually signed by all member countries. Rather than a verbatim adoption of the German approach, however, each country remained free to tailor its own interpretation of the law with differing priorities according to local needs. Germany, the Netherlands, Denmark, and Finland, for example, placed more emphasis on refillable and returnable systems. France, in contrast, recognized reuse, recycling, and energy recovery (through incineration) as equally preferable methods of waste reduction. In addition, the percentage-based waste targets adopted by mem-

Extended Producer Responsibility Symbol. The Green Dot symbol, introduced in the early 1990s in Germany, was more than a sign that a package was recyclable. It also demonstrated that a fee had been collected to pay for the package's end-of-life disposal.

ber states have varied widely as have their abilities to economically and effectively achieve recovery goals.

Over the past decade, disparities in interpreting and implementing the packaging directive have resulted in occasional diplomatic wrangling, with a few cases still in the courts. Some allegations charge that strict quotas on refillable containers intentionally disadvantage faraway small producers within the EU. For example, German supermarket chains have been accused of dropping French mineral waters from their shelves in an effort to meet their own country's mandate for refillable containers.

Overall, however, EPR legislation has had the intended effect of moving up the waste stream into product and packaging design, logistics, and shipping departments of major manufacturers. Consumers have also been brought into the process. According to Anne Chick of Kingston College, Europe's EPR legislation has forced numerous companies to rethink their packaging design and delivery systems in ways that actually improve the bottom line.[64] Liquid household cleaners and many cosmetics, for example, have increasingly switched to concentrates and refill systems. The use of PVC blister packs has declined in favor of single-content paperboard. Hooks for hanging products have been integrated into the packaging, thereby eliminating double packaging. These and other solutions generally result in lower Green Dot manufacturer fees.

The packaging ordinance converted Germans into a nation of sorters and recyclers, and after less than a decade nearly 20,000 companies had registered their products with the Green Dot.[65] The system, however, has not yet created a closed-loop economy for packaging. In fact, many feel that the gains made in the early years of reform could now be in a slow state of reversal, with both recycling and packaging on the rise. Writing in *Whole Earth* magazine, Sara Bloom, an American living in Heidelberg, Germany, cites two primary reasons: increasingly stressful lives in which convenience products play a significant role; and rising consumption, driven, at least in part, by a sense that the ability to recycle a package justifies any level of purchasing.[66]

However, Aktion Unverpack, an extreme subcommittee of the Bund (the German Federation for Environmental and Nature Conservation), has waged a new antipackaging campaign—"*besser nackt als verpakt*" ("better naked than packaged")—to pique consumer consciousness.[67] New legislation was slated to impose mandatory deposits on all nonrefillable beverage containers in 2003 in order to meet refill quotas,[68] but that legislation has stalled for a number of reasons. Retailers have protested that the costs are burdensome and the program will decrease sales. Manufacturers challenge that refill mandates discriminate against foreign producers.[69] This clearly points to the multitiered obstacles to legislating resourceful purchasing habits.

An Emerging Global Standard

Germany's packaging ordinance released the proverbial genie from the bottle, and its influence and complexity, while still relatively recent, is transforming packaging and solid waste policy throughout the world. As of late 2003, 31 countries had adopted or were considering take-back laws on packaging. According to Michele Raymond of Raymond Communications, a Maryland-based publisher of global recycling law resources, "Lawmakers in most countries [outside the United States] do not even question whether there should be some form of national 'take-back' law for certain products, but rather what form makes the most sense."[70] Thus, EPR legislation has moved beyond Germany's borders to new EU member-states like Poland and Hungary as well as to Argentina, Brazil, Uruguay, and Canada and to Pacific Rim nations confronting their own landfill crises—Japan, South Korea, and Taiwan.

Deeper changes are now under way. Bans on specific packaging materials are creeping into producer responsibility legislation. Taiwan has banned the free distribution of plastic bags and disposble plastic dishes in order to combat an unsustainable overflow of plastics, also known as "white pollution." South Korea has created empty-space ratios to enforce packaging efficiency. The South Koreans have also limited certain types of multilayered packages and set up bans on certain PVC and expanded polystyrene foam materials.[71]

Despite a world of differing approaches, this first wave of EPR programs share a number of basic commonalities:

1. EPR extends the manufacturer's responsibility from the design and marketing to the post-consumer stage. (In some countries, the costs of disposal and recycling are shared by government and industry.)
2. Producers either physically take back and recycle their own products or pay a third party to do so.
3. Individual governments set requirements for specific recycling targets, define what counts as recycling and waste, identify hazardous substances to be avoided, and require their own data collection and reporting.
4. EPR is moving beyond high-volume, low-value transactions such as packaging to include longer-term single purchases such as electronics and electrical goods, batteries, cars, tires, and other products.

The costs of lightening packaging's share of the total solid waste burden have not been inconsequential. This has led some critics to argue that imposing high waste-recovery targets—without thoughtful integrated analysis—has artificially shifted one set of resources to save another. According to one source, €5 billion were spent to recover just 1 million tons of household packaging in the year 2000.[72]

The Expanding Face of Extended Producer Responsibility

Begun in 1991 in Germany, EPR legislation—also known as take-back laws—has steadily gained acceptance as a means of reducing packaging and raising fees for collection and processing. By 2004, Norway, Switzerland, all EU member states and accession countries, as well as a growing number of Pacific Rim states had adopted some form of EPR for packaging. The United States remains formally opposed to the legislation, although a number of states have bottle bills. Many other countries are considering various types of EPR proposals as well.

EPR Adopted		EPR Under Consideration
Europe	Poland	Argentina
Austria	Portugal	Brazil
Belgium	Romania	China
Bulgaria	Slovakia	Mexico
Cypress	Slovenia	South Africa
Czech Republic	Spain	Tunisia
Denmark	Sweden	Turkey
Finland	Switzerland	Ukraine
France	United Kingdom	Uruguay
Germany		
Greece	**North America**	
Hungary	Canada	
Ireland		
Italy	**Asia**	
Latvia	Australia	
Lithuania	Japan	
Luxembourg	New Zealand	
Malta	South Korea	
The Netherlands	Taiwan	
Norway		

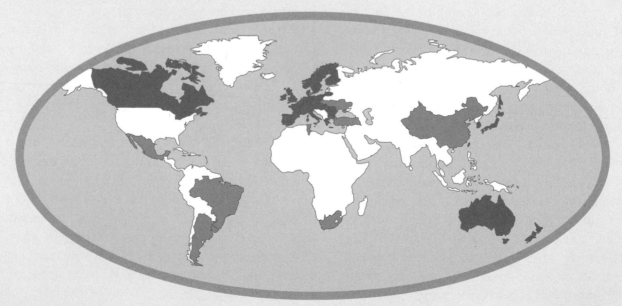

Source: *Environmental Packaging International, 2004.*

Paper or Plastic

Furthermore, among EU countries, the costs and effectiveness of packaging wastes has also ranged widely. The Netherlands has been heralded as one of the most efficient nations at recovering wastes of all kinds. This is attributed primarily to an integrated industrial policy that fosters shared responsibility across manufacturers, distributors, collectors, and others throughout the entire product life cycle.[73] The Dutch approach to extended producer responsibility may be worthy of careful study by other countries. The cost of recycling a ton of packaging waste in the late 1990s was nearly five times greater in Germany than in the Netherlands.[74]

The Rising Bar

With nearly 10 years of experience behind it, in 2003 the EU engaged in negotiations to dramatically strengthen and harmonize the standards of the packaging directive. In addition to raising waste-recovery targets for material classes through 2008 (between 55 and 80 percent of all packaging categories will have to be recovered), the EU has moved toward establishing more specific (and hence, controversial) "essential requirements." These are six far-reaching parameters intended to harmonize design standards to facilitate maximum recovery in all countries. These evolved standards call for the following: (1) Materials must be separable and recoverable, rather than simply theoretically recyclable. (2) Degrad-able packages must be organically recoverable. (3) Packages earmarked for incineration must burn safely and effectively with a measurable positive energy production. (4) Manufacturers must prove that a package solution can't be smaller. (5) Packages must be free of noxious substances and hazardous materials. (6) Reusable packages must be specified whenever possible.

EPR is also rapidly progressing beyond the packaging sector and into the total product chain via take-back programs. In the case of electronics and electrical goods—whose production and rapid obsolescence imposes solid and hazardous waste burdens on communities throughout the world—ongoing efforts are transferring the responsibility for the recovery of cell phones, computers, monitors, and other electronic goods to the original manufacturers. Automobiles are next in line, with end-of-life vehicle legislation in the EU aiming for an 80 percent recycling rate by 2005.[75]

Will the United States Join the Global Community?

The United States remains a major holdout in adopting EPR legislation. Perhaps its bureaucratic apparatus insults the country's spirit of *laissez-faire* and voluntary participation. Others challenge whether the actual environmental benefits warrant costly mandatory recovery programs. (In the words of one skeptical American industry insider, "Why should we have to pay for the right to collect corrugated? We shouldn't have to pay 90¢ to recover 10¢ of value.")[76] Instead, the U.S. Environmental Protection Agency promotes a hierarchy for waste management that calls for: (1) a reduction in the municipal waste stream at all levels; (2) recycling as much as possible, including composting; and, as last resort, (3) waste-to-energy incineration or landfilling.

Businesses pursuing international trade, however, increasingly face the need to comply with the rest of the world's EPR packaging requirements. For global corporations like Starbucks, whose business is rapidly expanding throughout Europe, complying with EPR standards is causing design and packaging procurement teams to rethink packaging strategies. "This may soon affect the standards for all of our packaging," explains Margaret Papadakis, a packaging buyer for the Seattle-based multinational coffee retailer.[77]

While U.S. corporations would be wise to consider voluntarily adopting the essential requirements as their own standards for environmental responsibility, many corporations maintain two distinct systems—one for EPR countries, and one for the U.S. market. On an encouraging note, however, California passed a take-back law on electronic goods in 2003, requiring a disposal fee on all lead-bearing computer monitors as well as a phase-out of heavy metals used in consumer electronics. This is seen by professionals like Marissa Juhler, of the company Waste Management, as a sign of things to come: "This is a first for the United States, and we hope it leads the way for us to join the rest of the world in holding corporations accountable for their crucial role in managing solid waste."[78]

In an ideal world, change would occur without the need for a legislative stick or intricate bureaucracies. But, in many countries, landfills are enormously unpopular and local budgets too strained to effectively deal with the solid-waste stream. Packaging take-back laws have certainly contributed to elevating the standards for designing products that are less toxic, less overpackaged, longer lasting, and specifically intended for reuse and recycling. EPR laws provide a procedure to hold accountable those parties with the greatest ability to reduce environmental and human health impacts—the ones who design, make, advertise, and distribute them in the first place. These responsibilities, however, should not be limited to packaging waste but should apply to all participants across the entire product chain, from cradle to cradle.

Finland's Bottle Law: Countrywide Standardization

In their excellent resource *Thinking Green: Packaging Prototypes 3*, Edward Denison and Guang Yu Ren report that Finland currently enjoys the lowest rate of packaging waste per capita among European countries.[79] The authors attribute a great deal of the Finns' successful waste reduction to the broad-scale standardization of beverage and transport packaging systems. All take-out soft drinks and alcoholic beverages produced within the country, for example, must be packaged in returnable bottles. (Consumers pay a deposit that is refunded upon return of the bottle.)

This one packaging ordinance has fostered an environment of both competition and cooperation among soft drink and beer producers who are forced to simultaneously stand out and conform to design parameters. But it seems to be working. Refillable plastic and glass bottle shapes have become standardized, and suppliers are adapting to uniform washing and refilling machinery. Of the approximately 650 million liters of beer and beverages consumed in the country each year, Denison and Yu Ren reported, over 90 percent are packaged in returnable, refillable bottles. Wine and liquor bottles also enjoy a 70 percent refill rate.

A similar program has established nationwide reusable transport packaging for the distribution of fruits and vegetables. Although reusable containers are primarily used to pack locally grown produce, even imported foods that normally arrive in corrugated containers are repackaged in reusable ones. Of the 1.2 million tons of packaging materials generated yearly by Finland's five million citizens (excluding corrugated cardboard), over 800,000 tons are reused.

One might argue that such an autocratic system is only possible in a small, relatively isolated region, and that it comes at a high price to society. However, it can no longer be said that uniform packaging requirements unduly handicap business as usual. Economies are dynamic and can be quick to adapt.

Source Reduction: Packing More with Less

Source reduction—minimizing materials, energy, and waste—has become a rallying cry as well as an economic imperative for businesses and industries alike. Reduction is, after all, the first of the proverbial "3Rs" (reduce, reuse, and recycle). And source reduction is probably the single most effective strategy that businesses can adopt right away to reduce solid waste. The reasoning is fairly simple. A package designed to be as efficient or contain as much recycled material as possible can actually have less impact than a package that is totally recyclable but never finds its way into a reprocessing system. (This is not, however, an argument against developing the regional infrastructures necessary to effectively recover and process all wastes.)

"Dematerialization" and reuse have become the primary pathways to source reduction, embodying a number of differing strategies and outcomes. A package or its elements can be eliminated. The product itself can be reformulated or redesigned. For example, a liquid can be reformulated into a concentrate; a bottle can be changed from a one-way to a refillable container; or a desktop printer might be made more robust to withstand shock during transit. High post-consumer recycled content materials can be substituted for virgin feedstock. A lighter material can be chosen to save on materials, water, and energy (related to manufacture and transport).

Source reduction is frequently quantified with the following goals in mind:

- Reducing the weight and volume of packaging entering the waste stream
- Reducing the amount of packaging materials used without compromising quality and/or performance
- Reducing package weight, thereby saving energy related to transportation
- Optimizing the amount of packaging materials associated with unitized loads
- Reducing energy consumption through efficient manufacturing and handling processes
- Avoiding waste through good product protection in storage and distribution
- Supporting suppliers who recycle waste and by-products from package manufacturing processes

Weight Watching

Keeping the amount of packaging materials to a minimum has always been a sound business strategy. And to that end, packaging converters are continuously redesigning, recombining, and recalibrating materials without our realizing it. Much has been written, for example, about the engineering feats that have optimized wall thickness designs and shaved between 25 and 50 percent off the weight of single-use glass, aluminum, plastic, and paperboard containers without sacrificing packaging strength. Between 1970 and 1998, aluminum beverage cans were trimmed down from 21 to 12 grams, a 43 percent weight decrease. The number of beverage cans yielded from 1 ton of tinplate grew by 50 percent—from 24,000 to 32,000—between 1985 and 1998.[80] Glass bottles (both traditional milk containers and soft drink varieties) have also experienced similar weight declines over the past two decades.

By doing away with a shrink-wrap on bulk-product boxes, California-based Clif Bar eliminated 90,000 pounds of plastic, saving $445,000 each year.[81] In collaboration with the Alliance for Environmental Innovation, the shipping company UPS redesigned its overnight envelopes to include 80 percent post-consumer waste in the late 1990s. This move supported less-polluting manufacturing systems, used the waste stream for supplies of raw materials, helped conserve energy, and set an example for the rest of the industry. Perhaps even more important, the alliance followed up this initiative with a program to improve the fuel efficiency of yet another major freight carrier, the Federal Express vehicle fleet.

The Ups and Downs of Lightweighting

Considering the long-range transport of single-use containers, it is generally accepted that lighter is better, since less cargo weight translates into energy savings and lower overall materials costs. This practice, known as "lightweighting," is behind many packaging decisions made today, with plas-tics emerging as the material of choice, since they are lighter and more flexible than heavier, more rigid counterparts.

Examined from a systems perspective, however, lightweighting can become a slippery slope with a number of downsides that counteract its benefits. Because they are cheaper to ship, lighter packages promote longer-distance transport and thereby compete with regional products. Lighter packages are increasingly made from flexible plastics that are seldom recycled or are nonrecyclable. Their compactability leads to more landfilling and incineration. Finally, the relative low costs of lightweight virgin plastics stand in the way of the development of more resourceful, refillable, and returnable systems.

Consider the case of Stonyfield Farm. Each year, this New Hampshire–based dairy company sells 8-ounce cups of organically certified yogurt by the millions. To get those single-serving containers from its East Coast distribution center to retail outlets throughout the United States, Stonyfield requires a complete "product delivery system" that includes containers, lids, inner seals, a paperboard and film multipack, as well as secondary corrugated boxes, shrink-wrap, and transport pallets.

In attempting to optimize its packaging solutions, Stonyfield engaged the services of the University of Michigan's Center for Sustainable Systems (CSS), which conducted a thorough life-cycle analysis, concluding that, in terms of present practical packaging solutions, lighter is better. The challenge is that, in this case, the lighter package is a #5 polypropylene cup. This resin is manufactured without the use of chlorine, unlike some other plastics, a definite benefit. Unfortunately, #5 polypropylene is not recycled in many communities, a situation that annoys a number of Stonyfield's ecologically motivated loyal customers. In fairness to Stonyfield, however, while the next best plastic alternative, HDPE #2, achieves a recycling rate of 24 percent, this applies to bottles but not to widemouthed yogurt containers (of which less than 2 percent are presently recycled). Although polyethylene bottles and cups share the same material, they have different melting points. So in this case, lightweighting saves material and energy related to transport, but it means that much of the material is presently destined for the landfill.

The most surprising finding to come out of the CSS study was that, in packaging yogurt, the larger the container, the lower the environmental burden. Simply switching from 8-ounce single-serving cups to 32-ounce bulk containers would allow Stonyfield to save 27 percent of the energy needed to package its product—an equivalent of 11,250 barrels of oil annually. This, of course, reinforces the notion that source reduction begins at home. Those quart containers have already been drastically dematerialized, having lost 30 percent of their package weight in the past 10 years. Through optimizing consumption, maximizing bulk purchases, and supporting local producers, consumers can put themselves on the front lines of source reduction—as long as purchasing in bulk doesn't result in an increase in wasted food.

To their credit, both Stonyfield and the CSS recognize the limits of lightweighting and dematerialization, and they look forward to an era of more radical improvements to Stonyfield's ecological footprint. Establishing an additional yogurt production facility closer to non–East Coast markets was proposed to further minimize impacts related to transportation. Biodegradable materials could potentially address the landfill issue, with the introduction of a compostable or edible cup. Designing the primary package for maximum strength could help reduce the amount of corrugated secondary packaging. And in a nod toward abating landfill impacts in the short term, Stonyfield has encouraged customers to collect and send back their used containers (cleaned, of course). These are passed on to Recycline, a company that incorporates them into the handle of the Preserve toothbrush, which contains various other recovered materials as well.

Toward a Refillable and Lightweight Frontier?

As William McDonough and Michael Braungart have persuasively argued in *Cradle to Cradle*, focusing only on marginal reductions in the amounts of materials, toxins, or harmful processes—"being less bad"—only slows the inevitable consequences of environmental degradation.[82] As relatively small as the overall packaging burden may seem, in a world of six-plus billion people, our daily purchases add up.

One optimal direction is to combine source reduction with closed-loop packaging systems. Designing a refillable container to be as strong and lightweight as possible, for example, is one possible way to accomplish this. A variety of refillable bottles are now made from PET, polycarbonate, or other materials, taking the place of heavier (and more costly to ship) glass for milk, bulk water, and other products. These can be used dozens if not hundreds of times, decreasing transportation costs all the while, before ultimately being recycled. Ideally, these lightweight containers will also be designed and remanufactured without harmful plasticizers, catalysts, and other "bad actors."

Motorola: Featherweight Solution

In its quest to ship fragile, silicon wafers between its production centers in Scotland and the Far East, Motorola has enlisted the ultimate source reduction agent—air. Faced with exorbitant shipping costs and unsustainable breakage rates, company designers ultimately decided to abandon their single-use corrugated and slotted polyurethane in-fill packaging solution. In its place they developed the Air Cushion package, a custom stacking and inflation system. Covered with integrated circuits, the wafers themselves are thinner than a human hair. They can, however, be stacked in neat packs like solid blocks. The Air Cushion buffers a series of interlocking containers (that hold the wafer stacks) inside a durable pouch inflated with air or nitrogen to a pressure of 1.25 pounds per square inch. An integrated handle on the pouch allows for its easy placement inside a corrugated box. Upon arrival at its destination, the Air Cushion is deflated, the internal containers removed, and both are returned to Scotland for reuse. The Air Cushion's inflatable pouch has a seven-trip life cycle. The internal wafer containers can be reused 25 times. Since its implementation in late 2001, wafer breakage has been virtually eliminated, material use has been cut by 75 percent, and air freight charges have declined by nearly 75 percent.

Hewlett-Packard:
Take Away the Package
to Lower the Damage

It's a supreme understatement to describe Hewlett-Packard as a leading supplier of desktop printers. As of early 2002, the global electronics giant was selling an estimated three to five million printers per month. Typically, these printers are assembled in one location but are composed of various parts from various places, all separately packaged. Once assembled, they are then shipped to central distribution centers and from there out into the world in individual packages. Each box requires approximately 14.6 square feet of corrugated cardboard, not to mention ink and adhesives, foam cushioning, and peripheral printed matter, adding up to a mind-boggling monthly flow of raw materials. At one time, before changing its graphics, the company estimated that it spread nearly 5 square miles of ink per day to imbue its boxes with the distinctive white-and-blue image. According to Paul Russell, Hewlett-Packard packaging process manager, each year the company spends in excess of $350 million on packaging alone.[83]

Kevin Howard is a senior packaging designer with the company, whose academic focus was on the shock absorption capacities of packaging materials. He has since spent years in the trenches addressing the monthly challenges of transporting and boxing millions of desktop printers. "There are very good economic and ecological reasons to consider the package as an inherent part of the product," says Howard, who earned both a B.S. and an M.S. in packaging science from Michigan State University. "For one thing, the more durable a product is, the less vulnerable it will be to shock damage during shipping. And the more compact the design, the greater number of units that can be stacked on a conventional pallet-sized shipping platform."

For that reason, Howard and his colleagues in Hewlett-Packard's Vancouver, Washington, design offices sit down with mechanical engineers to discuss shipping dynamics early on in the product design phase. For example, the addition of a few reinforcing ribs on the printer itself created a stronger product that in turn reduced the materials needed to protect it during distribution. "You have to balance product robustness with package protection and the hazards of distribution," says Howard, explaining a number of ways printer packaging has been reduced.

One of the standard myths Howard subscribed to was that the box had to support the load when shipping the product from the manufacturing facility to the distribution center. But, he said, "We found that when items are boxed, people have the tendency to throw them around or run into them with forklifts. Boxes actually invite damage. So we eventually decided instead to ship products without one."

Howard then exchanged the standard wood pallet and individual box system for cavitated polystyrene foam trays stacked five high, all set atop a plastic slip sheet. The entire refrigerator-sized bundle was then shrink-wrapped. "We found that the ability to see the fragile products through the clear shrink-wrap made the handlers more cautious than they were before with an inexpensive box obscuring the contents. Our damage rates decreased, our loadability increased about 2.5 times, and we began to save significantly on transport costs. The moral of this story is that by taking away the package you can lower the damage," says Howard. "But most people still insist a box is necessary for shipping products long distance."

For cushioning materials, Hewlett-Packard specifies expanded polystyrene foams containing no CFCs. Howard insists they have determined the optimal amount of cushioning material to use. And he considers die-cut corrugated boxboard a tough trade-off as an alternative shock absorber because it requires more materials to perform the same job. This means bigger individual boxes and more pallets. "You can't be too narrowly focused," says Howard. "If foam goes to the landfill, it compresses effectively. If corrugated is re-pulped, there is still considerable loss and the resulting sludge may also have to be landfilled. It's a very precise balance that requires a lot of thought and engineering."

Some of the other materials Howard is investigating are Regale molded pulp (see page 104), sealed air cushions, die-cut corrugated, and shock-absorbing cushions made from recycled milk jugs. An obvious business opportunity is the establishment of small mills, located near assembly facilities, that transform the packaging materials (used to transport components) into new products such as building or packaging materials.

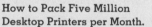

How to Pack Five Million Desktop Printers per Month. By replacing individually boxed and palleted desktop printers with a stackable system of foam trays and shrink-wrap, Hewlett-Packard packaging engineers lowered damage rates, decreased material needs, and increased loadability.

Aveda: Optimizing Post-Consumer Content and Beyond

How does a company engaged in the fiercely competitive health and beauty products industry move beyond paying lip service to environmental concerns? At Minneapolis-based Aveda, which has developed one of the world's most enlightened packaging programs, it starts with the commitment of founder Horst Rechelbacher and president Dominique Conseil. Along with upper management, they encourage employees to continually improve the environmental performance of both their products and their packaging. Granted, Aveda (a $500 million autonomous subsidiary of the Esteé Lauder corporation) faces the challenge of being a global company that sources, manufactures, and ships products from continent to continent. This means that any gains in environmental performance must be viewed against the backdrop of international transportation impacts, packaging materials that need to be large enough to accommodate multiple languages, raw material sourcing policies, and other concerns. Still—in a business where image is everything—Aveda uniquely surfaces as a company that proactively ranks environmental packaging goals above short-term pricing and sometimes even aesthetic considerations. Any company interested in serious packaging reform can benefit from a study of their policies and achievements.

Breaking the Mold

Optimization best describes Aveda's approach to packaging design. For nearly a decade, the company has been dematerializing its packaging—by lightweighting containers as well as by maximizing the post-consumer recycled (PCR) content of plastics such as high-density polyethylene (HDPE), polypropylene, glass, and other materials. According to Mary Tkach, Aveda's director of environmental sustainability, product and packaging designers interact closely in order to find ways to continually increase the post-consumer content in all aspects of packaging, from primary bottles and squeezable tubes to secondary paperboard boxes and collateral materials.[84] Even their pallets and transport packaging have been addressed.

"Solutions can range from reformulating the product in a package to changing the packaging itself," says Tkach. A product might be made more liquid, so it could be bottled in a high PCR content HDPE container rather than a squeezable tube. One hundred percent PCR paperboard cover-stock paper might be specified for sleeves and cartons on some products. Or the secondary packaging could be eliminated altogether. In certain cases, the product could be modified. The natural essential oils that form the bases for most of the company's products, for example, are more active than synthetic oils. This has required careful testing and collaboration with suppliers to ensure that the package and the product are compatible.

Such work is time consuming. One critical obstacle can be finding suppliers who have the technology and willingness to push the envelope of post-consumer content. At times Aveda has accepted an increase in material costs in order to achieve its environmental goals, such as a rare 16 percent price increase to maximize the PCR content of an extruded tube package. Post-consumer materials haven't always commanded a premium, however, especially after the research and development has been completed. In fact, using high PCR content can be money saving despite a system heavily skewed toward virgin resource extraction. A 10-year effort to redesign shampoo bottles to make them as thin as possible and maximize the post-consumer resin content now saves the company about $1 million per year.[85]

Design Priorities

John Delfausse, vice president of packaging development, explains that Aveda's approach to maximizing post-consumer plastics content has evolved with experience, which, in turn, has informed a hierarchy of design priorities.[86] Aveda now actually ranks environmental performance ahead of cost and design concerns, even though all three are essential packaging considerations. "The first question designers ask is whether the material is recyclable," explains Delfausse. "A second priority is to build component parts out of a single material so that they can easily be sorted and recycled."

Plastics Hierarchy

The following illustrates Aveda's hierarchy when considering the use of plastic for packaging.

Most preferred:
High-Density Polyethylene (HDPE)
Low-Density Polyethylene (LDPE)

Acceptable:
Polyethylene Terephthalate (PET)
Ethylene Vinyl Acetate (EVA)
Polypropylene (PP)

Least Preferred:
Polyurethanes (PU)
Polystyrene (PS)
Acrylonitrile Butadiene Styrene (ABS)
Polycarbonates (PC)
Acrylic

Prohibited:
Polyvinyl Chloride (PVC)

Source: Aveda Corp. Material User Manual, as cited in "Wrap Artists: How Aveda Bundles Sustainability into Its Packaging," The Green Business Letter, December 2003, p. 5.

An official *Material User Manual* has been developed to guide departments through the optimization process. Aveda's "most preferred" resins are high- and low-density polyethylene (HDPE and LDPE). Polypropylene is an "acceptable" material, also favored by Aveda packaging designers. All three have fairly clean supply sources, consume comparatively less energy in manufacturing, and contain little or no toxic or carcinogenic materials. Even though it is highly recyclable, polyethylene teraphthalate (PET) is used only occasionally. It is avoided whenever possible because of the "bad actors" it contains such as antimony, a plasticizer used in the production process; when they do choose PET, designers specify the maximum post-consumer content possible. Out of the desire to avoid hazardous substances, the company has stopped using polyvinyl chloride (PVC) packaging altogether. (Esteé Lauder, Aveda's parent corporation, has taken a similar pledge.)

Achieving such high rates of single-material, post-consumer content has been a methodical process for Aveda. Concerned both about unintended interactions between the essential oils in its natural products that contain post-consumer plastics and about the printability and aesthetics of containers, Aveda originally sandwiched "junk" material between inner and outer layers of virgin plastic. Company designers worked continually with suppliers to increase post-consumer content incrementally, first with the outer printable layer, and later with the inner surface. Satisfied that maximizing recycled content was a totally acceptable and even desirable solution, Aveda now boasts the highest levels of post-consumer content packaging in its industry. Two decades ago nearly all HDPE was derived from virgin materials, but Aveda has succeeded in raising the PCR content in much of its packaging to between 80 and 100 percent, with very little containing less than 50 percent. Aveda has worked with 100 percent post-consumer newsprint molded pulp, 94 percent PCR glass, and even agricultural crop residues—the "shives" or straw from flax—blended with plastic resins for a lipstick container.

A Systems Approach

Caps, spray mechanisms, and multicomponent parts can be the bane of any environmental packaging designer who is attempting against all odds to fashion the ideal package made out of single, easily recyclable material. For that reason, Delfausse puts a great deal of thought into systems that might facilitate collection, or packaging "take back" or "leasing."

"Aveda needs upwards of 20 million caps per year," reasons Delfausse. "That's a lot of PCR material. A fairly simple infrastructure could be set up within our 200 retail stores and 6,000 salons to collect the caps. Unfortunately, in the past when we've tried this we've ended up with a lot of garbage." Still, Delfausse hopes to introduce a cap recovery system sometime in 2005 and is investigating the possibilities of in-store refill stations as well.

In addition to its own internal design guidelines, Aveda relies on a software program called Merge for further qualitative analysis. Developed by the Boston-based Alliance for Environmental Innovation, a project of Environmental Defense, Merge scores and rates products and packages on a series of metrics: packaging resource consumption; packaging energy consumption; virgin materials content; nonrecyclable materials content; presence of known toxins; greenhouse gases; and pallet efficiency.

"Balancing the costs and trade-offs of packaging can be extremely complex," says Tkach. "Is it better to use a 50 PCR/50 virgin (chlorine-bleached) paperboard or to use a 20 PCR/80 virgin (non-chlorine-bleached) paperboard? The key is having good information and a framework to analyze those options."

That the company has succeeded in achieving such high rates of PCR content without compromising the product should send a clear message to the rest of the industry. Post-consumer plastic, however, is not necessarily transparent. One of the challenges of designing packages with high PCR content is adjusting to a minimal graying in color. "Everybody from the president on down had

to accept that the bottles' color turned slightly grayer," says Delfausse. "But by doing it, we save about 150 tons of virgin polyethylene on an annualized basis."

Beyond Confidentiality

While occasionally compromising on higher materials costs and accepting a slightly abbreviated color palette may seem questionable practices for many corporate capitalists, it is Aveda's stand on confidentiality that is perhaps most unusual. The company doesn't view its hard-won environmental R&D discoveries as proprietary trade secrets. Instead, it has gone out of its way to advertise them, sponsoring meetings with suppliers and sharing material research with numerous injection molders. Favored suppliers have frequently been revealed in articles and Web site reports—Johnson Printing for cartons and sleeves; ALCAN Packaging and Owens Illinois for bottles; CCL Plastics for tubes; TricorBraun and Kaufman Container for bottles, jars, and caps. A few manufacturers have taken notice and made the switch.

"One of our goals is to enable other companies to carry on with the work of these new materials," says Delfausse. "The sooner others can get started, the better off everyone will be."

Ben & Jerry's:
Getting the White Out

"I guess I'm the eternal optimist," says Andrea Asch, manager of natural resource use for Ben & Jerry's Homemade, speaking of the two-and-a-half-year R&D effort it took to develop the company's "Eco-Pint." "Sometimes you have to be content to take on one single issue at a time rather than solving an entire industry's packaging problems overnight," says Asch, a veteran of corporate environmental affairs.[87]

The fact is that developing the 100 percent, non-chlorine bleached, virgin wood, kraft paperboard container, introduced in late February 1999, was just the first phase in a long-term overhaul of the conventional ice cream container—the pint. (The Eco-Pint is made of virgin wood as required by law and still goes to the landfill because of its petroleum-based vapor and moisture barriers.) Ben & Jerry's researchers and packaging designers immediately started searching for alternatives to the federally mandated food-grade internal polyethylene coating, the second most significant element in the pint packaging. The outside of the package has a standard clay coating with a titanium dioxide tint (for crisp graphics). Other details, such as inks and glues should follow, with the ultimate goal of making the package both chlorine free and biodegradable.

Work on the Eco-Pint initially stemmed from a single goal—eliminating chlorine from the company's packaging. One might think the simple change from white to brown paperboard would be an easy one, but it was a long, uphill battle. Outside consultants and nongovernmental organizations helped the company identify key issues and options. The company put the pieces together. "We embarked on a global search for the right kind of paperboard," notes Asch. The hunt eventually led to Atlanta-based Riverwood International's unbleached kraft paperboard mill. Riverwood uses lodgepole pine as its primary feedstock, sourced from various suppliers, and the switch required a fair amount of fine tuning. Just being able to curl the lip to precise dimensions, for example, posed challenges for the manufacturing team. The company absorbed an upcharge in the start-up phase, but the cost of bleached paperboard has since risen while the price of unbleached paperboard has declined.

"We would love to make an FSC-certified container in the future," explains Asch, speaking of the international certifying agency that offers third-party chain-of-custody accreditation for sustainable forestry (see page 94). "But FSC-certified wood is not our story at the present time," says Asch. "We're focused on the elimination of chlorine and chlorine-bleached materials."

The industry status quo for packaging ice cream entails using chlorine-bleached paperboard coated on both sides with a petroleum-based vapor and moisture barrier. What stands between the recycling bin and your treasured pint of ice cream is a thin coating of polyethylene film that keeps warm air out and the cold ice cream in. Finding a nonsynthetic and therefore compostable solution for the vapor and moisture barrier is the next phase of the packaging project. "If we can get away from landfills and create dynamic systems such as compostable living solutions, then packaging can be part of that vision," says Asch. "In that case, one company's byproduct could become another's raw material." In this case, from pint to soil. Of course, the old-fashioned sugar cone is the ultimate ice cream package: totally edible with a simple unbleached wrapper.

In an ironic twist, not long after Ben & Jerry's (now a wholly owned subsidiary of Unilever Corporation) launched the Eco-Pint, a complaint was filed with the Federal Trade Commission alleging that its environmentally friendly packaging was misleading, since the ice cream tested positive for dioxin residues. Laboratory tests revealed that its World's Best Vanilla flavor, which the company used to launch its new packaging, contained 0.70 parts per trillion of dioxin.[88] Rather than taking away from Ben & Jerry's effort, the finding seems only to affirm that dioxin-producing industrial processes must be abandoned, as these carcinogens travel unimpeded through the air and water, moving up the food chain, causing potential harm. Even a product as seemingly (yet arguably) wholesome as ice cream can become contaminated, and that contamination can be linked back to paper and packaging production, among other causes.

Upstream in the production process, Asch has also been working to develop returnable packaging systems for ice cream ingredients. Disposable 5-gallon pails that contain cherries, for example, have been replaced by a metal bin and liner system. Each reusable bin holds over 1 ton of fruit; only the inner plastic liner is thrown away. Similar reusable packaging solutions are being applied to ingredients such as caramel, eggs, bananas, and marshmallows.

Natural Systems Design

It is hard to imagine the bicycle, the helicopter, or even the deep-sea-diving apparatus as the design inspirations of a 16th-century genius acclaimed more for his painting masterpieces than for his scientific inventions. Leonardo da Vinci had the rare capacity to envision and design objects far beyond the technological capacities of Renaissance society. Much has changed in the centuries between da Vinci's Europe and today's global industrial consumer society. The design and marketing of everyday things has emerged as one of the most powerful tools shaping the world around us, as they trigger a cascade of events and social forces that coalesce each time a finished product comes into being. Yet despite the undeniable escalation of material comforts in nearly every aspect of daily life, one has to question whether basic items—from kitchen utensils to computers—and their packages shouldn't require more forethought, intention, and context before being birthed into material existence.

"In an environment that is screwed up visually, physically, and chemically, the best and simplest thing that architects, industrial designers, planners, etc. could do for humanity would be to stop working entirely," said the late Victor Papanek, author, professor, and early advocate for environmental and social responsibility within the design professions. "But it seems to me that we can go beyond not working at all and work positively."[89] As Papanek rightly pointed out, designers can be a threat to society, particularly when their design decisions are made without an understanding or concern for the environmental and social systems in which their creations function. Conversely, design can become a catalyst for change.

Taking up that mantle, a legion of interdisciplinary thinkers are calling for a new industrial revolution, one based upon a design imperative that merges ecology, economics, and the pursuit of vital human communities. Individually and collectively, these thinkers envision nothing less than a radical transformation of the ways in which we provide goods and services, from agriculture and architecture to everyday products and, yes, packaging.

A Short History of Natural Systems Design

"Natural systems design," the term I have chosen for this broadening movement, is known by a variety of names—industrial ecology, eco-design, design for environment, and green design, among others. Its history reaches at least as far back as the master designers of the British Arts and Crafts Movement in the mid-1800s, to the Bauhaus School, Frank Lloyd Wright, and Buckminster Fuller, to a generation of modern practitioners swept away by Rachel Carson's *Silent Spring*, E. F. Schumacher's *Small Is Beautiful*, and the *Whole Earth Catalog*. Austrian-born Papanek's seminal work *Design for the Real World: Human Ecology and Social Change* appeared in 1971, railing against cheap goods designed for rapid obsolescence. He decried the need for an ethical design that honored the environment and served the poor, disabled, and elderly. Papanek followed up in 1995 with *The Green Design Imperative*, which was widely read and highly acclaimed.

Over the past century, numerous authors, designers, and others have attempted to establish new parameters and lenses for environmental design. Their ideas are increasingly gaining currency within businesses and the mainstream media. Such visionary thinkers, however, may share the same fate (though perhaps not the same overabundance of talents) as da Vinci—that is, they might be at loggerheads with the powers that be. They are envisioning ways of producing, distributing, and recycling goods and materials that could ultimately conflict with the massive scale and operating conditions of global capitalism. While designers may wield significant authority, they also work within complex social and economic arrangements. The real challenge, therefore, lies in creating products on a case-by-case basis that facilitate meaningful, incremental change. It may take decades to develop such innovations, but, in the meantime, they point the way toward blueprints for reform.

Natural systems design is predicated on the notion that working with Nature—or producing goods and services in the cyclical manner that Nature does—is ultimately the only true path we can forge toward "sustainability." In this age of cell phones, nanotechnology, and global production networks, it is admittedly a challenging notion. Perhaps our most striking examples of such design and production systems can currently be found in conservation-based agriculture, or green architecture. Cropping systems that are uniquely tailored to their local landscapes, like grass-pastured livestock in areas of abundant rainfall, shade-grown coffee farms in mid-elevation tropical forests, or high-diversity organic farms in productive valleys, exemplify "natural systems farming." Another model would be a residential or commercial building carefully sited and designed from low-impact, regionally sourced materials configured to filter rainwater runoff and optimize passive solar energy for heating, cooling, and lighting.

The Designer as Activist

Natural systems designers use their powers at the onset of the product planning process to become catalysts for a new economic paradigm—one beyond open pit mines, clearcut forests, factory "farms," effluent pipes, smokestacks, squandered one-way resources, mounting landfills, and grungy sweatshops. By creating products and markets for a new economy, the designer can, at least in part, help to generate positive feedback loops for such important social and environmental forces as renewable sources of energy, diverse and biologically safe materials, healthy ecosystems, and empowered human communities. Businesses, consumers, and government all stand to benefit in the long term.

For the designer, "natural systems" becomes the operative term. Products, materials, and manufacturing processes are analyzed within the entire life cycles in which they originate and operate. Once informed, the designer becomes an optimizer, balancing environmental and social objectives along with variables of function, production, cost, aesthetics, and marketability. Wastes, including inefficiencies, are proactively combatted. Hazardous substances and endangered resources are avoided in favor of more environmentally benign alternatives. One-way, disposable designs are replaced with an ethic of durability. Products may be designed to be returned to the producer at end-of-life or to reenter various post-consumer production streams either as biological elements (safely biodegradable) or as easily separable and recoverable technical nutrients (mineral or synthetic materials). Finally, an educational relationship is set in motion, engaging both producers and consumers.

A natural systems design approach demands a fundamental change in the way we perceive of design's relationship with the economy, the Earth, and communities around the world. In addition to mastering the basics of any design field—form, function, aesthetics, engineering, business, and so on—it requires a commitment to unraveling the complete product histories of everyday things. For packaging designers, crossing over into other disciplines and pools of knowledge for inspiration and

up-front research could involve visits to cardboard mills and plastics converters, attendance at forestry summits, or trips to landfills. For companies committed to voluntary responsibility and corporate leadership, it could result in the establishment of environmental design manuals, interdepartmental design and production green teams, membership in intra-industry or industry-wide improvement initiatives, and so on. This active engagement also demands an ongoing and forthright assessment of success criteria and a commitment toward continual improvement.

Design for Assembly, Multifunctionality, Edibility, Reuse, and Disassembly

A natural systems designer can start with a conceptual framework based on the many Rs—reduce, reuse, remanufacture, recycle, recover, rot, regionalize, reinvent, and so on. They reinforce the important upfront role that designers and manufacturers play both in the building of markets for recycled materials and in reducing raw materials and energy.

For years, designers from many fields have been gleaning the packaging waste stream for clean sources of post-consumer material. In 1993, Patagonia revolutionized the sportswear industry when it co-developed a post-consumer recycled synthetic fleece material called Synchilla. This process converts two dozen spent PET soda bottles into a plush, high-value garment. In just 10 years,

Patagonia alone has diverted nearly 100 million bottles in the production of fleece pullovers and other garments. And even though synthetic fleece has become a global standard, two-thirds of the 40 billion plastic bottles consumed in the United States each year still end up in landfills.

Recovered packaging materials can also be converted into building materials. In Monterey, Mexico, Rastra blocks are manufactured by grinding polystyrene packaging planks into tiny beads, mixing them in a slurry (80 percent foam/20 percent cement), then molding that mixture in forms. The resulting blocks are highly insulative, relatively lightweight, insect- and rot-resistant, and designed to interlock. After they've been stacked and their inner channels intertwined with rebar and filled with concrete, the Rastra blocks help create a long-lasting, thick-walled, monolithic structure that can be stuccoed or plastered inside and out. Similar recycled material/cement block

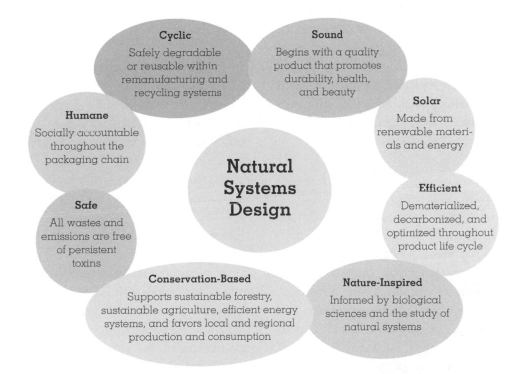

Cyclic
Safely degradable or reusable within remanufacturing and recycling systems

Sound
Begins with a quality product that promotes durability, health, and beauty

Humane
Socially accountable throughout the packaging chain

Solar
Made from renewable materials and energy

Natural Systems Design

Safe
All wastes and emissions are free of persistent toxins

Efficient
Dematerialized, decarbonized, and optimized throughout product life cycle

Conservation-Based
Supports sustainable forestry, sustainable agriculture, efficient energy systems, and favors local and regional production and consumption

Nature-Inspired
Informed by biological sciences and the study of natural systems

systems are being made from ground-up pallets and waste wood.

By now, most of us have heard of the straw-bale house. In Korea, the husks that protect rice kernels are also being considered a valuable resource. Rather than being composted or burned, these silica-rich husks can be processed into packaging materials for electronic goods on their way to Europe from Korea. Once on the continent, the rice husk packaging can be reused as insulation fibers, added as a flame retardant stabilizer for bricks, or encapsulated into particle board. According to author and chemist Dr. Michael Braungart, as the rice husks travel from farm-field castaways to factory packaging to commercial or residential building material, they are "upcycled" to a higher value, longer-lived product at each stage.[90] As of the writing of this book, a German university held the patent on this process.

Total Beauty

British environmental design consultant Edwin Datschefski writes that, as a consumer society, we must transcend "the hidden ugliness of an ordinary day."[91] Such ugliness, he says, is manifested in the 30 tons of waste—gases, pollutants, and copious other ecosystem violations—incurred during the manufacture of each ton of product that eventually reaches a consumer. The antidote to hidden ugliness, he believes, begins with designing products around the principles of "total beauty." Datschefski arranges these into five major design criteria:[92]

1. Cyclic (capable of safe decomposition or closed recycling and remanufacturing loops)
2. Solar (derived from or powered by renewable energy)
3. Efficient (durable, optimized for material and energy consumption, multifunctional, and so on)
4. Safe (wastes and emissions are toxic-free)
5. Social (embodying the principles of fair trade and the social accountability standard, SA 8000)

In addition to examples of everyday products, Datschefski provides useful frameworks for designing, rating, and researching products that are 100 percent cyclic, solar, and safe. Among these is a rudimentary system that calculates "UglyPoints" on a material basis, as well as techniques for establishing a long-term plan for continuous improvement.

Natural Capitalism

It is a strange world indeed in which jobs created from a tragic oil spill cleanup, rising health-care costs due to deteriorating air quality, or a boom in building materials due to postwar reconstruction are calculated as positive economic indicators. It is a stranger world still that omits from the balance sheets the essential services to human economies supplied by healthy forests, clean oceans, productive farmlands, and other thriving ecosystems. Social entrepreneur and author Paul Hawken has spent over a decade attempting to debunk an economic system that fails to adequately account for the environmental costs and social inequities of predatory business practices. In his latest book, *Natural Capitalism*, Hawken, along with coauthors Amory and Hunter Lovins (cofounders of the Rocky Mountain Institute), value such services as carbon sequestration and cycling, water and air purification, soil protection, habitat preservation, climate regulation, pest control and pollination, and energy production to be in excess of $36 trillion per year. This is nearly the equivalent of the entire annual gross world product.[93] The authors call for the replacement of the "first" Industrial Revolution—based on the exhaustion of those invaluable yet finite resources—with a humane and ecologically intelligent one they call "natural capitalism." Such an economy would be driven only by the interest on what Schumacher termed the planet's "natural capital": renewable energy and resource flows generated daily and yearly by natural ecological cycles.[94] Rather than economic growth fueled by depleting fossil fuels and ancient ground water supplies, by overharvesting fisheries and forests, or by destroying topsoil and mineral reserves, they advocate the birth of a conservation economy. Companies, engineers, designers, and others are called upon to contribute to a world

where unprecedented levels of efficiency make the most of available sunlight, energy, local materials, human labor and ingenuity, and other forms of natural capital. Principles of natural capitalism include:

1. Increasing the productivity of resource use by exponential leaps
2. Shifting to biologically inspired production models (biomimicry)
3. Moving from products to services in order to generate solutions-based business models
4. Reinvesting in natural capital

C2C: Cradle-to-Cradle Eco-Effectiveness

The now-famous phrase "cradle to grave" outlines the typical trajectory of a consumer good or package on its way to the landfill. Eco-designers William McDonough, a Virginia architect, and Michael Braungart, a German chemist, deny that such a waste-bound life cycle is benign or that anything ever really goes "away," including the 80,000 defined chemicals and mixes in use today. Design, they argue, has an ultimate purpose—the pursuit of ecologically appropriate, socially just, and economically viable "cradle to cradle" (C2C) solutions. C2C design solutions, for example, might include a building that processes its own wastes and produces more energy than it consumes. Fabrics and packaging materials that safely dissolve back into organic forms would be another example of C2C design. "Eco-effective" industrial systems where "waste" from one activity creates "food" for another material or process form the underlying core of C2C design. In a May 2003 story in *Packaging World* magazine, the authors suggested a number of strategies for eco-effective packaging:

1. Designing only with "biological nutrients" that can be safely reabsorbed into water and soil or with "technical nutrients" that can be continually upcycled in closed resource loops

2. Carefully selecting inks and additives so that packaging materials can be easily recovered, effectively recycled, or safely incinerated

3. Using as much material as necessary to protect and differentiate the product but also ensure a resourceful afterlife for the packaging

4. Designing packaging with materials and amendments so that littered wraps could potentially decompose into soil nutrients

5. Creating low-priority postage systems to recover materials[95]

Cradle-to-cradle design had inspired McDonough and Braungart's popular book by the same name as well as their design studio, which consults with Fortune 500 companies, and, more recently, a Charlottesville, Virginia–based nonprofit organization, GreenBlue, established to facilitate the adoption of these principles within industries. Among GreenBlue's ongoing projects is the Sustainable Packaging Coalition, formed in late 2003.

GreenBlue has organized and hosted a number of design colloquia with representatives ranging from paper and resin manufacturers to consumer product companies and government agencies. The Sustainable Packaging Coalition has begun to develop its organizational strategy and plans to introduce a universal definition for sustainable packaging in 2005. Among its early projects is "intelligent materials pooling," a collaborative initiative to foster the closed loop recycling of materials such as polyethylene and bioplastic PLA (polylactic acid).[96]

Biomimicry

Rather than relying on hard chemistry for ready answers, can packaging designers, engineers, and others learn from the way spiders spin webs, how leaves generate color, what makes a pelican's pouch elastic, how organisms naturally freeze and thaw, or the way mollusks generate shells and coatings? Janine M. Benyus, biologist, design researcher, and author of *Biomimicry*, argues that we can steer ourselves toward sustainable manufacturing systems by using nature as the model, mentor, and measuring standard of our design solutions. By imitating the ways in which organisms and ecosystems generate products and create and process wastes (such as a prairie's ability to provide its own sources of fertility, nutrient cycling, pollination, and pest control), biomimicry advocates believe our industries and economies can (and must) be reinvented. Of course, most things in nature are packaged for local and short-term distribution. The essay "Packaging Tips from the Porcupine Fish (and Other Wild Packagers)" (see pages 76–79) explores how biomimicry might inflence packaging.

Breaking Through the Green Wall

Hurdles of all kinds stand in the way of implementing natural systems design. For example, there are up-front costs in time and resources needed to develop new expertise and alternatives. Unfortunately, the onus usually falls on motivated manufacturers and distributors, because the packaging industry lacks a serious commitment to research and development, particularly where the environment is concerned. For companies that persevere, however, the extra initial investment in human capital and product development can be made up in real profits as new designs carve out previously untapped savings.

Perhaps the biggest obstacle, however, is the supremacy of marketing priorities: eye-catching graphics, brand visibility, trendy materials, and ever-increasing "added value." Designer Anne Chick, author of *The Graphic Designer's Greenbook*, refers to this as the "packaging dilemma." According to Chick, packaging design is more often driven by decisions about branding and marketing than about solving environmental problems. "In order to break through the green wall," says Chick, "eco-designers usually have to pitch ideas that save money or meet legislative compliance, rather than those that support real on-the-ground innovation."[97] To that end, no amount of design philosophy will stimulate environmental reform. Design and marketing briefs must demand it in the first place.

Celery Design Collaborative:
The 80 Percent Solution

"Myth: Designers are powerless to create environmental packaging solutions." So declares Brian Dougherty, founder of the Celery Design Collaborative in Berkeley, California. "It's easy for designers to fall back on the status quo and choose whatever is cheapest. Adding ecological design qualifications definitely raises the work load a bit," he says, "but it's totally within reason—not to mention the increased job satisfaction."[98] By way of example, he cites the choice of something as basic as inks.

An essential element in most graphic applications, inks also spread an environmental burden. They comprise three basic ingredients: a pigment that carries the color; a vehicle that allows the pigment to be applied; and binder that attaches the pigment to the printed surface. There are two primary concerns. First is the use of heavy-metal pigments like barium, copper, and zinc used in particular colors—certain warm reds, fluorescents, and metallics. Second is the widespread use of petroleum as the pigment vehicle. "For the most part, these metals are not harmful to people in their normal use on printed packages," says Dougherty. "But they tend to linger around and can end up polluting water that leaches from landfills, concentrate into toxic ash from incinerators, or become toxic sludge in a pulp de-inking facility."

One solution, says Dougherty, is to keep handy a list of Pantone colors listed under the U.S. Environmental Protection Agency's Section 313 of Title III of the Superfund Amendments and Reauthorization Act. This identified certain inks that contain potentially hazardous levels of heavy metals such as barium, copper, or lead. Users are required to report the release of these metals when certain thresholds are exceeded. Avoiding colors with heavy metals altogether means disqualifying approximately 20 percent of the Pantone color palette. Dougherty asserts that, while obviously limiting, it is relatively easy to specify a slightly different color with a less-toxic pigment.

Also Recommended . . .

● **Choose vegetable-based inks.** Most conventional inks have a petroleum vehicle or base. Despite the detrimental consequences of industrial agriculture, soybean, canola, cottonseed, and other vegetable oils are currently the preferred options. Research your choices carefully, because many inks can contain both vegetable and petroleum bases. In fact, an ink can contain more than 90 percent petroleum and still qualify for the SoySeal trademark label.

● **Choose low VOC inks** (less than 10 percent). Another issue associated with an ink's base concerns volatile organic compounds (VOCs). Highly volatile inks set and dry quickly on the printed surface. While speeding up production time, these VOCs can be unhealthy for workers in the press room and release ozone-depleting molecules. Soy-based oils contain between 1 to 10 percent VOCs, whereas petroleum-based inks contain 25–40 percent VOCs. Specifically ask for Low VOC inks (less than 10 percent).

●**Choose food-grade inks.** An increasing number of inks have been developed for the food industry, meaning they are approved for direct contact with food and skin. See www.colorcon.com/ for more details.

Pantone Colors with Pigments Containing Section 313–Listed Chemicals

Regular			Metallic		
Color Range	Color Range	Color Range	Color Range	Color Range	Color Range
123–26	1765–1815	490–95	8001–5	8680–82	8820–22
136–40	183–88	497–501	8521	8700–02	8840–41
1365–1405	189–95	4975–5005	8540–41	8720–22	8860–62
150–54	211–16	504–9	8560–61	8740–42	8881–82
1555–1615	436–40	5185–5215	8580–82	8760	8900–02
163–68	443–47	5535–65	8600–01	8762	8921
1625–85	455–57	560–65	8640–41	8780–81	8941–42
170–75	4625–45	567–72	8660–62	8800–01	8961
176–81	469–72				

Reds and Metallics. The main toxicity problems in inks lie with warm reds and metallic colors. Reds often contain barium, which, if inhaled, can lead to lung irritation, and when absorbed can cause spasms and even heart problems. Metallic inks include copper and zinc compounds, which can also cause skin, lung, and eye irritations, as well as allergies in some people. When degraded, these compounds can also move through the ecosystem. Barium-free and nontoxic matches can be found for most but not all colors.

Source: Eco Newsletter 8, no. 4, published inside Communication Arts magazine, May/June 1999.

All trademarks used herein are the property either of Pantone, Inc. or other companies.

Packaging Tips
from the Porcupine Fish
(and Other Wild Packagers)

by Janine M. Benyus and Dayna Baumeister

From ancient pottery to plastic tubs, the trend is clear: we're a species that totes, stores, and shields our treasures from a capricious world. And we're not the only ones. Skins, auxiliary pouches, and egg and seed cases do exactly what our commercial packaging does: contain loose items, protect from the outside world, and connect to the outside world via surfaces that signal. Given the similarities, what might we learn from other organisms about packaging with the least effort and no regrets? This process of asking our biological elders for sustainable advice is called "biomimicry."

Packages That Contain

● **Expand and collapse.** Many of life's containers are flexible, like the throat pouch of the Clark's nut-cracker that expands to hold 150 pine-nut-sized seeds, or the pelican pouch that scoops 3 gallons of seawater at a swipe. What if we could design a juice bottle that would fill up like a sturdy balloon, then collapse to a small disk when its liquid is gone? You could store it in your pocket as a go-cup, or send hundreds back to the manufacturer in a single envelope.

● **A cellular matrix.** Fruits and vegetables are bottles that don't slosh because their liquid is stored in and between cells. By weight, carrots are 92 percent water; lemons, cucumbers, and tomatoes are 96 percent water; and lettuce tops them all at 97 percent water. What if we were to store precious or even dangerous liquids in such a cellular matrix, so that a puncture was not a crisis? Or how about using a cellular matrix for the skin of a bottle? An empty bottle could be eaten like an orange slice, and a bottle of shampoo could dissolve in the bath instead of lingering in the landfill.

● **Optimal packing.** Gaze at the face of a sunflower, the seeds of a pine cone, or leaves spiraling around a twig, and you'll see packing refined to an art. Leaves and seeds are arranged in what mathematicians call the Fibonacci sequence (each number added to the one before gives the next number: 1 1 2 3 5 8 . . .). Fibonacci spirals in seed heads allow uniform packing at every growth stage, with no crowding in the center and no sparse patches at the edges.

Packages That Protect

● **Grace under pressure.** A great place to look for impact resistance is in the rock and roll of the tidal zone, where soft-bodied creatures like snails, barnacles, and mollusks brave the waves. Their shells self-assemble from minerals in the sea water through a process called "bio-mineralization." There are at least 60 kinds of biomineralized materials, including the abalone's mother-of-pearl, which is an organic/inorganic composite that's twice as tough as our high-tech ceramics. To add toughening organics to our hard-shell packages, we'd have to forsake our kilns and take up the art of low-temperature self-assembly.

Scrapes and falls. For scrape-free packaging, we'd be wise to ask snakes, whose hardened folds of keratin (scales) seal out water, provide flexible traction, and buck constant abrasion. To coddle fragile items, we might consider the strategies of seed helmets—nuts. The highly reinforced, three-layered Brazil nut pod defies opening from all but its ally, the agouti, a caching rodent with strong, specially angled teeth.

Just-in-time protection. Nature's packaging is rarely overbuilt. The pliable sea cucumber's skin stiffens just when it needs to—when struck by a predator, for instance. Imagine being able to pack items close together in their softer form, using far fewer materials in less space, and still being assured that, if the box drops, the packaging will become rock hard.

Another responsive packaging idea comes from porcupine fish. Their spines are set into the skin, erecting only when the fish is threatened. To trigger the inflation, they sip tiny gulps of water. A package that started to fall might be induced to puff up in the same way with air, bouncing on spines when it hit the ground.

Self-repair. Our bodies are packages within packages. Every cell has a fatty membrane that self-assembles when placed in water, then reassembles when a breach occurs. Imagine a polymer wrapper that would heal when ripped during use, but would eventually decompose when placed in a compost heap. Models for this "timed degradation" are everywhere in the natural world, including the varnish-like sealant that covers the byssus tether of the mussel. Tough on microbes when in use, the sealant becomes vulnerable after two years, when the mussel no longer needs the thread.

Protection from microbes. To protect against microbial squatters, a biomimic would look for clues in the skins of organisms that manage to keep themselves slime-free. Red and green algae (kelp) are able to stabilize a normally reactive compound called bromine in a way that fends off microbes without harming the alga. Nalco engineer William McCoy borrowed this stabilization recipe to create Stabrex, a chlorine alternative that keeps industrial cooling systems microbe-free. Other models for antimicrobial excretions include olive trees, biscuit roots, lichen, and fire ants.

And then there's always the good bacteria/bad bacteria strategy. When good bacteria occupy niches, bad bacteria struggle to get a foothold. It's why lactobacillus helps in your digestive tract, and why adding good bacteria to surgical wounds keeps bad infections at bay. Could we bring ourselves to create a favorable environment for good bacteria, and actually welcome them as watchdogs in our packaging?

Protection from air and water.
Seed cases are champions of air-
and water-tight storage. Among the
record-holders: a lotus that germinated after 1,288 years; a Polynesian
box fruit that germinated after two
years at sea; and the Mary's bean,
a liana seed that traveled from the
Marshall Islands to the beaches of
Norway, more than 15,000 miles!

Steal this package. Imagine a
thief grabbing a package encased in
slime, and you begin to see what
makes the eel-shaped hagfish so
predator-proof. (To remove its slime,
the hagfish ties itself into a knot and
moves the knot along its body.) Bacteria, slugs, fish, and several
amphibians and reptiles also secrete
slime wrappers. While not recommended for gift packaging, it may be
a slick strategy to protect goods in
the warehouse, before retail.

Failing on purpose. Another interesting take on natural protection
comes in the form of sacrificial layers
like those in a horse's hoof. The outer
layer is designed to slough off under
pounding pressure, exposing the next
layer of new hoof. Shaggy or platy
tree bark is also sacrificial; fast-mov-
ing fires crisp the outside layer of
cedar or ponderosa pine, then smol-
der to a stop. Perhaps our outer packages should be designed to burn or
break on purpose, dissipating stress
and shielding the goods within.

The ultimate dematerialization
might be to shuck the package altogether, and make wear-and-tear an
asset as it is in beaver's teeth. What
if we agreed that products got better
in transport and handling, the way
sandblasted jeans or distressed
leather does?

Packages That Connect

Active interfaces. Skin bristles
with sensing and regulating
devices, opening pores to help animals stay cool or raising goose
bumps to lift thermoregulating hairs.
Leaf pores automatically open to
exchange gases when the sun
shines, and they close tight when
the leaf needs to retain water vapor.
"Smart packages" like these would
be a godsend in the produce section, or would help with the transi-
tion from refrigerated trucks to hot,
humid warehouses.

Berries go on sale. Fruits and
berries are masters of focus-
grouped advertising—-they are
specifically colored to attract the
birds, mammals, and even fish that
will best spread their seed.

The ripening process is highly
orchestrated as well, with berries
staying an unappetizing green, and
without much sugar content, until
the seeds are fully grown. Once
seeds are ready, berries actually go
on sale, heightening their color and
sugar content, and becoming irre-
sistible to impulse shoppers. Imagine if our packaging had a color
change that signaled a sale to help
move the inventory before it
became stale.

Expiration past due. Another
boon to retailers would be food or
drug packages that announce their
impending expiration dates with a
color change. In plants, it's the oxidation of limited lifespan pigments

such as anthocyanin that turn flower petals brown. Oxidation also accounts for the browning of scored apples. Perhaps a similar coloring mechanism could alert retailers to bruised boxes.

● **Going my way?** A winged seed puts up a sail so that wind currents will carry it to distance soils, and burrs cut down on shipping costs by hitchhiking. Might we design more products for co-packaging with related products, or shape our packages to ride in buses, subways, or ferries going there anyway? If packaging was reimagined, what else could we dispense in the vending machines or in-store displays that are already in place?

What Waste?

Nature's packages are designed from the get-go to return to natural cycles. There's also an inherent multifunctionality in nature's materials that we have yet to master. Take the seven-layered candy wrapper, for instance. The "75-gauge polypropylene/ink/adhesive/60 gauge metallized-oriented laminate" provides mechanical protection, moisture control, ease of opening, and brand declaration.

But the insect cuticle does all this in one material—-a composite of polysaccharides whose functions are achieved by altering the shape of the polymers, their alignment, and how they are bonded together. Since chitin contains only four ingredients—carbon, hydrogen, oxygen and nitrogen—shaped into tasty molecules, its afterlife is mercifully short.

How Organisms Make Packages

And last but not least, the manufacturing of life's packages is also a benign affair—-chemistry performed in water, using local raw materials, powered by current sunlight, at body temperature, and without toxic chemicals.

With the right models and the right humility, we might just be able to learn from the form, the process, and the ecosystem fit of life's packaging. When we finally get it right, we can tip our hats to our mentors, take a bow ourselves, and join the ranks of other organisms that package without harm.

Janine M. Benyus and Dayna Baumeister direct the Biomimicry Guild, a nonprofit research and education center. The Biomimicry Guild seeks to study nature's models in order to solve human design problems. Contact: P.O. Box 575, Helena, Montana, 59624 or www.biomimicry.org.

Wood Reduction:
Packaging and the Fate of the Forests

Leda Huta contributed significantly to this section.

Forests have served as a primary source of packaging materials for as long as human beings could wrap things in bark or fashion wooden boxes, crates, coopered casks, and kegs. But it was really late-19th-century advances in papermaking technologies—which subsequently led to the chipping and pulping of the world's forests throughout the 20th century—that set off a rapid escalation in wood-based packaging. Since then, materials derived from wood have done a great deal of the heavy lifting in the packaging of our present-day consumer society.

Paperboard cartons, corrugated cardboard boxes, transport pallets, molded pulp cushions and trays, paper labels and instruction manuals, shock-absorbing filler materials, shipping envelopes, cable spools, and much more contribute to making wood-based products the largest sector of the municipal waste stream. It should come as no surprise, then, that forests across the world are under massive assault from global industrial timbering operations filling the supply lines for wood and cellulosic fibers. These include the boreal forests across northern Canada and Siberia; temperate forests in the southeastern United States, Canada, South America, and Siberia; and tropical and subtropical forests throughout Indonesia and Latin America.

The Gifts of Healthy Forests

Our rapidly urbanizing and wood-consuming human population often takes for granted the significant benefits of a world graced with healthy forest ecosystems. Intact forests support some of the highest levels of biodiversity on the planet as well as being home to hundreds of millions of people living in indigenous communities that depend on them for their survival. In addition to providing mostly far-away populations with lumber, wood chips, pallet stock, fuel wood, and tonewoods for musical instruments, forests generate a number of "nonwood" essentials. Medicines, mushrooms and mycillial networks, spices, fragrances, foods, oils, and recreational and spiritual values are all quantifiable and qualifiable forest products and services. More important, forest ecosystems fulfill essential ecological functions such as native habitat, water purification, soil stabilization, carbon sequestration (the in-take of toxic carbon dioxide into plant tissues), and protection against natural disturbance events.

All told, the immense benefits of these complete "services" must be carefully weighed against the volume of wood resources a forest provides. Considering that these annual nontimber values have been estimated in the trillions of dollars,[99] it is arguable that logging is the least productive use of a forest's resources. For example, in southern Australia, hundreds of thousands of people are losing the ability to drink their water because it has become too salinated as a result of the industrial clearing of forests. Thousands of people have died in China in recent years from floods exacerbated by logging. And, blinding dust storms, attributed in part to deforestation and overgrazing in Asia, have induced respiratory problems such as asthma among residents of Mongolia, Central Asia, and even the western United States as these enormous storms cross the Pacific Ocean.

The timber industry frequently argues that, because wood is a theoretically renewable resource, our current levels of consumption and technological means of harvest are justified. Clearcutting, the standard harvest method used in most parts of the world, is often heralded as a technique that mimics natural catastrophes such as fires, floods, and blights. Another often-voiced reasoning is that there are more trees today in certain regions of the world than there were 100 years ago. These arguments, which reduce the world's diverse forest ecosystems to "wood baskets" of standing timber, have been challenged by foresters, university professors, and scientists for decades.

Meanwhile, the pace of industrial logging has accelerated at an alarming pace. According to the World Resources Institute, only 20 percent remains of the world's original ancient forests large enough to maintain their inherent biodiversity.[100] The vast differences between these biologically intact forests and heavily logged regions or tree farms cannot be underestimated. Even if trees are replanted following industrial harvests, previously diverse and complex forest ecosystems are usually replaced with plantation-style monocultures of fast-growing exotics. The regimen of clearcut and plantation conversion results in biologically simplified, even-aged stands of trees that are highly vulnerable to wildfire, disease outbreaks, and other naturally occurring events and often are incapable of supporting previous levels of biodiversity. In some cases, such efforts are failed almost from the start. Plantations in the Canadian boreal region, for example, are often completely wiped out during wind storms, because the trees cannot develop the interdependent root system networks they need to survive the harsh northern climate the way that virgin forests there have done for millennia. Infrastructure development such as roads ensure that these forests will increasingly become subject to further human development.

Similar activities are taking place across the globe at dizzying speeds. During the first decade of the North American Free Trade Agreement, forests in various regions of Mexico have been heavily logged to produce packaging for the burgeoning maquiladora industries. Plantation conversion in Latin America is predicted to grow 70 percent between 2000 and 2010, with Chile and Brazil leading the charge.[101] The southeastern United States has experienced a dramatic escalation of remote-capacity chipping operations, as timber corporations shifted away from protected areas in the Northwest and Northeast. Watersheds and ecosystems have been severely affected in the move to convert forests into industrial products (such as building materials, paper, and pallets) and replace them with monocultures of exotic pines.[102]

Protecting the remaining ecologically healthy primary and secondary forests should undoubtedly become a top priority in this century—if not for the love and sake of biodiversity, then for our global security. Without a simultaneous decline in wood consumption, however, forest protection in one area simply shifts the burdens of resource extraction to another region. Consider the case of California, which expanded the amount of its forestlands under protection by 60 percent over the past 15 years but did little or nothing to actively reduce consumption. The Golden State now accounts for 15 percent of the country's consumption of wood and paper—of which 75 percent is imported.[103] At a watershed 1996 gathering, the San Francisco–based Rainforest Action Network and a coalition of leading non-governmental organizations issued a radical plea for a 75 percent reduction in the consumption of all wood-based products (including paper, building materials, packaging, and fuel wood) in order to protect a worldwide matrix of healthy forests in the 21st century. How both conservation and consumption reduction can be simultaneously accomplished remains an enigma of serious proportions.

Types of Wood-Based Packaging

● **Paper.** This material has been a packaging industry workhorse for nearly a century because of its myriad uses, minimal storage requirements, relative ease of processing, and other advantages. The mass production of collapsible paperboard boxes developed in the late 1800s ushered us "inside the box" and literally revolutionized our world. Paper consumption more than tripled between 1961 and 1998, with packaging accounting for the largest segment—nearly half of all paper. Globally, paper packaging consumption has risen more than three-fold since 1960, despite advances in dematerialization and the substitution of alternatives (primarily plastics) for wood-based packaging. Today, more than 600 pounds of paperboard are consumed per person annually in the United States—almost half of all packaging by value and more than half by weight.

Writing about the pulp and paper industry, scientist Allen Hershkowitz has said:

> Perhaps no industry has forced more species into extinction, destroyed more habitats, and polluted as many streams, rivers, and lakes. It is a tragic irony of commerce that paper, perhaps the most ubiquitous and ephemeral of all consumer products, is manufactured by destroying timber forests, one of nature's most durable and biologically essential organisms.[104]

● **Containerboard or corrugated box materials.** These are made by sandwiching a thick wavy or fluted sheet of paper between two flat sheet plies. One attribute of the corrugated box is that it can be reprocessed a half dozen times before suffering critical fiber loss (that lost sludge is normally landfilled, however). Corrugated can also be recycled just about anywhere in the world, unlike plastics, which are nonuniform and are normally downgraded if reprocessed at all. For these reasons, old corrugated containers have become one of the most highly recycled materials over the past 15 years, with collection and recovery rates hovering around 70 percent in the United States. As boxes are repulped and processed, however, wood fibers eventually disintegrate, and for issues of both strength and printability, most containerboard boxes typically contain a higher percentage of virgin rather than recycled fibers. In more advanced mills, those virgin-wood sources can be derived from "pre-industrial" wastes such as sawdust, cut-offs, and other byproducts of the construction and furniture industries. In addition, the adhesive lignin that bind wood fibers together can be extracted from chips and burned in order to generate steam energy that fuels the processing.

More than 90 percent of consumer wholesale and industrial goods are still shipped in corrugated cartons, which are usually used just once before disposal. Despite its high recycling rates, corrugated still ranks high among top categories in the municipal solid-waste stream, along with food, unpainted wood, and paper. Boxes soiled with grease, like the millions of take-out pizza flats used around the world every day, or boxes coated with wax pose severe problems for recyclers and are usually landfill-bound. (Some municipal landfills are beginning to ban corrugated, however.)

● **Boxboard.** This thin, lightweight, ubiquitous carton material is often used as secondary packaging for such items as toothpaste, aspirin, breakfast cereals, and so on. The enhanced printability of boxboard has at least partly fueled an escalation of this material for myriad applications. Unlike corrugated, not all boxboard contains a high percentage of recycled fibers even though post-consumer content offers a cost-competitive alternative.

● **Solid-wood packaging materials.** These are known in trade lingo as SWPMs. Pallets—used for stacking and transporting products across continents and communities—are the most prolific of this category and are a plague on U.S. forests. (Other SWPMs include cable spools, crates, and packing blocks.) According to Michael Hicks, trade policy coordinator for the USDA Foreign Agricultural Service's Forest and Fisheries Products Division, there are approximately two billion pallets floating around the U.S. distribution stream at any given time.[105] Building the 500 million replacement pallets needed to replenish that "fleet" each year consumes 40 percent of all hardwoods and 10 percent of all lumber cut in the United States.

Often the products of shoddy workmanship and low economic value—it's hard to say which is the driving factor—the majority of pallets are made for just one trip. Typically, they are either landfilled or ground into chips for incinerators, landscaping materials, or papermaking. On a volume basis, the estimated square footage of those annually discarded one-way pallets is enough to frame 300,000 average-sized houses.[106]

Large retailers—the organizations who arguably have the greatest ability to manage fleets of reconditioned pallets—have for the most part been reluctant to assume responsibility for more resourceful transport packaging solutions. One clear exception in that world, however, has been Home Depot. In 2000, Atlanta-based Home Depot engaged the services of multinational pallet recycler CHEP, which has provided Home Depot with a "returnable transit packaging" system for its 1,500 stores and 60 distribution centers across North America. CHEP sends Home Depot the pallets, which are then delivered to suppliers and later returned to the CHEP network for inspection and repair. According to one report, the 1.5 million reusable pallets recirculating in Home Depot's pool keep some 30 million pallets out of landfills on a yearly basis.

Further changes in the pallet world could be imminent, however. Landfills are clogging up in many areas, and landfill bans on items as useful as pallets could be one potential repercussion. Another confounding factor has been the spread, via pallet wood, of invasive insects such as the Asian long-horned beetle and pinewood nematode (also known as the pine sawyer). The Asian long-horned beetle is a wiry antennaed bug now gnawing its way through hardwood trees on various continents. Burrowing its way into pallet and crate wood primarily of Chinese origin, the globe-trotting beetle seeks out sugar maples, poplars, birch, and chestnuts, among

other preferred species, which it can kill within three short years of infestation. It has already caused the large-scale felling of trees in Chicago and New York City and, as of 1998, had been identified in 14 states.

Following the lead of agencies in Australia and New Zealand, international regulations are now in effect mandating that all globally traded containers either be fumigated, made from thermally or chemically treated wood, or derived from a nonhost alternative material, such as plastic, metal, plywood, or engineered wood. This spread of exotic pests signals a more toxic world for pallets, whether they are misted with pesticides, held together with synthetic adhesives, impregnated with an arsenic- or heavy metal–based treatment, or made of a petrochemically derived plastic.

Will the future give way to returnable transit packaging systems and highly durable pallets? Could we one day see a dual system with pallets for domestic markets and "exotic insect-free" SWPMs for international trade? If sweeping reforms are to take place, there's a lot at stake. In the United States alone, there are some 3,000 independent pallet makers closely tied with the hardwood industry. Whether or not these small outfits can abide by changing international regulations remains to be seen. In addition, pallet pools have already been around for some time in Europe and have not exactly taken the United States by storm. The logistics of creating and maintaining economically viable pallet pools face the main challenge of overcoming the vast distances that often separate production centers and distribution outlets. In the meantime, virgin-wood pallets still account for roughly 90 percent of the market, and far too many pallets end up in landfills.

●**Molded pulp.** This material is perhaps best known as the spongy and flaky material of grey egg cartons and bluish-purple apple trays. It is increasingly being used within boxes as a form-to-fit shock cushion. Originating as papier-mâché perhaps as long as 3,000 years ago, molded pulp got its modern industrial start in the early 1900s. Manufacturers of molded pulp became very early recyclers of virgin-wood-based papers, converting old newspapers and corrugated containers into their finished product. The high costs of making molds, combined with limitations in the depth, shape, and printability of potential forms, confined this type of packaging to a few niche markets. As a result, molded pulp was eclipsed by thermoformed foams and plastics, even though the latter cost more. In the past decade, however, molded pulp has experienced a resurgence. Benefiting from advances in technologies such as transfer molding and thermoforming, molded pulp is now graced with smooth, printable surfaces. With the public outcry over the nonrenewability of plastics not diminishing, molded pulp is being marketed as a renewable and highly recycled and recyclable alternative. It is used to cushion electronic products within cartons, as a base for trays glazed with high-temperature and moisture-resistant coatings, and even as a decomposable potting container for both ornamental plants and veggies.

●**Wood shavings.** Manufactured specifically to be used as a filler in shipping containers and gift baskets, wood shavings are often marketed as a "renewable, environmentally preferable" alternative to Styrofoam peanuts and other shock-absorbing dunnage or "bogus" fillers. The wood shavings generally derive from trees that were previously undervalued and referred to somewhat arrogantly as "junk species"—cut in larger logging operations, but unsuitable for other purposes. Their use as a packaging filler is an attempt to create a market for the victims of nonselective clearcut forestry practices. The forest products industry, however, is a mature market with a huge infrastructure for hundreds if not thousands of products that contain wood fibers. The danger in supporting yet another wood-based product like wood shavings is its potential to become a growing burden on forests in future years if the demand for the product signals substantial growth. The need could drive manufacturers to go beyond "junk trees" for sources of raw materials, exacerbating the pressure on forests. The term "junk species," furthermore, reflects merely the economic value of trees and not the many other benefits they may provide, such as food and shelter for wildlife, or their rightful place in the biotic community.

Wood Addiction: A Problem Long Ignored

The versatility of wood-based packaging, particularly paper, the lack of packaging ordinances in the United States, and the swell in consumer purchases from catalogs and the Internet spell a future crowded with packaging. Consider all the wood-based packaging used to ship a product ordered via the Internet. The product arrives in a corrugated box. The box contains a "filler" made of paper that has been shaped into any one of a number of creative designs—wadded, cut it into lattice patterns, crinkled—in order to cushion the product within the empty space. The actual product itself may then come in its own product packaging—a box, perhaps filled with additional papers describing the product or instructions for its use and another copy of the same catalog.

Sadly, reducing wood-based packaging has been the stepchild of the environmental community, addressed only as a part of broader campaigns. Only a smattering of public policies call for environmentally preferable packaging, and even fewer decry the need to reduce the environmental consequences of excessive wood-based packaging. As a result, American packaging designers, manufacturers, and buyers often lack the necessary information or incentives to reconcile their ecological footprint on the forests.

Although we have some packaging-reduction success stories—such as the high post-consumer content of packaging envelopes by UPS, Federal Express, and the U.S. Postal Service—on the whole, many U.S. companies are increasing packaging weights, expanding disposable packaging over reusable packaging, and adding nonrecyclable materials to packaging.

Governmental and Nongovernmental Attempts to Address Wood-Based Packaging

Driven by solid-waste crises and pressure from the New York Public Interest Research Group (NYPIRG), members of the New York State legislature have attempted to pass an environmentally preferable-packaging bill for nearly a decade. First introduced in 1993 and yet to be ratified, the Environmentally Sound Packaging Act calls for all packaging sold in New York State to be environmentally sound—reduced, reusable, recycled, or recyclable. The bill would require that within five years of enactment, a package would qualify as recycled only if it contained a minimum of 45 percent post-consumer recycled content. The bill also requires labels indicating the packaging's compliance with the bill. Unfortunately, heavy lobbying on the part of industry has continually defeated the bill despite repeated introductions by its sponsor; it has most recently been referred to the Environmental Conservation Committee.

At the same time that NYPIRG worked on the passage of the bill, it was also involved in a multi-stakeholder process to draft a model reduced-packaging bill. The process was overseen by the Coalition of North East Governors (CONEG) packaging task force. After two years of meetings, however, this attempt failed as well. (Nevertheless, CONEG's Source Reduction Council did successfully draft a model toxics-in-packaging bill that is now advocated through the Council of State Governments' Toxics in Packaging Clearinghouse. The primary aim is to phase out heavy metals.)

Federal legislators, meanwhile, have futilely attempted to address the issue of pallets. Senator Patrick Leahy (D-VT) introduced a bill in 1998 calling for a phase-out of all wood pallets imported into the United States. It was easily defeated.

Packaging is also one of the myriad products addressed through "green" purchasing initiatives. Under pressure from groups such as Ralph Nader's Government Purchasing Project (GPP), President Clinton issued Executive Order nos. 12873 and 13101, which, among other mandates, called on the federal government to minimize the environmental impacts of packaging. The U.S. Environmental Protection Agency then issued guidelines for "green" packaging purchases that delineate post-consumer recycled fiber content, such as 40 percent for solid fiber boxes, 75–100 percent for items such as pad backs, covered binders, and book covers, and 40–80 percent for folding cartons. Although most states have "green" purchasing policies for recycled paper, packaging is largely neglected. The GPP is working to make government purchasers aware that purchasing policies on issues such as packaging have tremendous impact on forest conservation efforts. Advocating reduced demand for wood products, the GPP calls on purchasers to implement strategies such as eliminated, reduced, and/or recycled packaging.

Massachusetts incorporates several environmental attributes, including in packaging, in its evaluation of vendors. A bidder that "greens" the packaging of its computers can gain extra points on its scorecard. (Massachusetts scores individual bids by assigning points to numerous attributes. In its computer contracts, for instance, bids are evaluated on environmental items such as toxicity, recycled content, upgradability, and other issues, such as years of experience and response time.) The packaging attribute encourages bidders to implement six environmentally preferable packaging strategies, calling for packaging that:

- Is made from recycled content that meets or exceeds federal and state recycled content guidelines (currently 35 percent post-consumer for all corrugated cardboard)
- Minimizes or eliminates the use of polystyrene or other materials difficult to recycle
- Minimizes or eliminates the use of disposable containers such as cardboard boxes
- Provides for a return program and location where packaging can be returned for recycling
- Has manuals printed on recycled-content paper that meets or exceeds federal and state guidelines for recycled content (currently 30 percent post-consumer content)
- Contains materials that are easily recyclable in Massachusetts

Vendors who meet four or more of these criteria receive 10 points for their packaging program on their bidder scorecard.

Seeing the Boxes for the Trees

At present, it seems doubtful that we can achieve anywhere near the 75 percent global wood-reduction rates that many experts believe are necessary to sever our march toward unrecoverable deforestation. Part of the reason is the complex nature of the challenges we face. A direct substitution of petroleum-based synthetics or farmed fibers for wood merely shifts the burden from one material base to another. Yet it is clear that much can be done, and that we should view our remaining biologically intact forests for what they truly mean to the biotic community: irreplaceable ecosystems to be preserved and restored as planetary treasures. As dire as the situation appears, some efforts can be taken to bring this predicament into balance:

● **Source substitution.** When regionally appropriate, intentionally grown fiber crops such as industrial hemp and agricultural residues—straw, corn stalks, and so on—can be substituted for wood-based fibers in bags, boxes, molded pulp, and filler materials. These can be processed in mini-mills that generally use less water, energy, and toxic chemicals and generate far less pollution than wood-based mills. (Universal Pulp in Eugene, Oregon, and Regale in Napa, California, are two such U.S. mini-mills that merit watching.) Tree-free stocks can be specified for instruction inserts and labels, or even blended with custom orders of high post-consumer recycled-content corrugated.

● **Source reduction.** The optimization of post-consumer waste fibers must become a global priority. This will require outright bans on all wood-based products from landfills, greatly increased consumer demand, and mandatory regulations on returning wood-based fibers to materials loops.

● **Source standardization.** Pallets should no longer be viewed as cheap, disposable, one-way packages. Standard sizes, durability requirements, and voluntary programs to manage pallet fleets could help stem this reckless abuse of resources.

● **Source avoidance.** Industries can take pledges (and adopt corresponding policies) to avoid using wood products of all kinds that are sourced from remaining ancient and biologically intact forests. For example, the British mill Universal Pulping, producers of Cullen Moulded Pulp, has taken a pledge to avoid hardwood-based or rainforest timber. (See Robert Cullen and Sons, Ltd., www.cullen.co.uk, for more details.)

● **Source protection.** Around the world, nations can direct tax dollars and incentives toward long-term conservation of remaining forests, creating a vital matrix of sylvan habitat across the earth. An initiative to place half of the Canadian boreal forest under "Forever Wild" protection, and to manage the remaining half under strict environmental guidelines for logging, road building, mining, and agriculture, is currently under careful review. The

Canadian boreal region constitutes one-quarter of all intact forest remaining on the planet and provides essential breeding habitat for nearly one-third of North American migratory waterfowl. (The World Resources Institute's Global Forest Index provides key information on global forest systems.)

● **Source regulation.** Third-party certification organizations, such as the Forest Stewardship Council, can provide essential checks and balances for on-the-ground management of working forests. This and other forestry initiatives can raise the baseline standards for long-term, sustainable management throughout the world.

● **Perception adjustment.** We must challenge the notion that wood is preferable to plastic because it is a renewable resource. All packaging production carries impacts, no matter how well certified or environmentally optimized. Our challenge is to make the best resource decisions possible for the long term.

● **Natural capital accounting.** Forests need to be valued in economic terms for the full range of benefits they provide to human and nonhuman communities. This would significantly alter the economic profitability of clearcutting, chipping, and shipping forests to industrial centers around the world.

The Benefits of Switching

Listed here are some of the benefits—and their equivalents—of switching to 35 percent post-consumer recycled content for medicine and cosmetics paperboard (based on 375,000 tons of annual usage):

Annual Benefit	Annual Equivalent
156,000 tons of greenhouse gas emissions avoided	Carbon dioxide emissions from 27,000 cars driven 200 miles a week
Wastewater reduced by 2.6 billion gallons	Wastewater from 27,000 households
510,000 fewer tons of trees used	Trees required to make the copy paper used by 11 million people
106,000 tons of solid waste avoided	Trash generated by 49,000 households

Source: Alliance for Environmental Innovation, "Greener Cartons: A Buyer's Guide to Recycled-Content Paperboard," November 20, 2001 (www.environmentaldefense.org/alliance/reports.html).

Third-Party Certification Organizations and EcoLabels

For the environmentally motivated consumer, the ecolabel has become a welcome (but sometimes confusing) addition to the now widely used recycling symbols on packaging. From coffee beans to pasta shells, office paper to building materials, mainstream products are being identified with a seal or stamp symbolizing that they've met some supplemental set of environmental and/or social production standards. Organically grown foods, sustainably harvested wood, shade-grown and fair-trade coffee, chlorine-free papers, sweatshop-free clothing, and predator-friendly wool and meats are just a handful of an ever-increasing number of market-driven, logo-based initiatives. It is a signal of changing values in the marketplace.

At their best, these ecolabels champion issues that government policies and market regulations have failed to adequately address. By uniting "responsible" producers with "concerned" consumers, these ecolabels initiate reforms for problems as diverse as human rights and fair wages, the protection of biodiversity, air and water contamination, and global warming. Producers proactively attempt to account for, as fully as possible, the upstream ecological or social consequences of labor, harvest, processing, and manufacturing. The marketplace becomes the arena where these "added values" either survive or fail.

Organic's Rising Star

The $36 billion global organic food industry has been the shining success story of the late-20th-century ecolabel movement. After a humble beginning in the early 1970s, the organic food movement blossomed into a global industry throughout the 1990s, achieving annual growth rates between 10 and 20 percent per year in the United States. While still a relatively small part of the industrialized world's food supply, organic foods are expected to capture significant shares by 2010—between 10 and 30 percent in some countries. Today, dozens of organizations around the world certify and market organically grown products. These organic labels have come to signify added values such as better-tasting and healthier food, a reduction in toxic pesticides, cleaner lakes and streams, and products free of genetically modified organisms. (With the increasing contamination of seeds through the drift of pollen from fields of genetically modified crops, however, this may eventually become impractical or impossible to guarantee.)[107] In the future, packaging may one day contain organically certified adhesives, inks and dyestuffs, protective coatings, or actual fibers such as industrial hemp, kenaf, cereal or grass straws, flax, or bagasse (sugar cane stalks).

The Rules of Success

All verifiable ecolabels share a number of commonalities. On the supply side, production standards must be established and codified. Production zones must be identifiable, with skilled monitoring teams in place to certify goods throughout their entire "chain of custody." This means from the forest or field through all processing stages to the retail shelf. Supply depends on a consistent base of producers willing to adhere to those standards and pay the costs of certification (including extra paperwork, marketing, and a willingness to be audited). On the demand side, outreach campaigns are needed to educate the public and attract a following of customers. In the retail environment, the package can play a key role—via a graphically striking label or concise message—since communicating the virtues of products requires extra effort in rising above the din of competition. This can be particularly challenging and frustrating when certified products command a premium. Challenging because consumers need to learn, at the point of purchase, the reasons for any added costs. Frustrating because conventional producers, who could potentially be guilty of contributing to biological or chemical pollution, are not compelled to reveal their product's—or its package's—detailed history.

As hard as it may be to build an ecolabel from the ground up, success can be one of its most critical challenges. Growth in the marketplace sooner or later becomes the driving gauge of achievement. Nonprofit foundations, which often rally behind and support the establishment of these initiatives, eventually expect ecolabels to operate solely upon the collection of certification fees. In order to expand both supply and demand, most certification organizations face inevitable clashes in goals between keeping production standards high and penetrating mainstream markets. Increased market share almost always means attracting larger producers. Unfortunately, as the industry grows, labels increasingly become the property of larger corporations who consolidate commodities for sale in the mass market. This growing process can be painful, especially when smaller, pioneering operations find themselves under-represented by the labels.

Successful ecolabels may also find themselves in the crosshairs of "free trade" enforcers. Perhaps the most high-profile example of this was Mexico's challenge to the World Trade Organization that the U.S. "dolphin safe" tuna standards impose unfair restrictions on its fishermen and therefore constrict markets.

Not All Ecolabels Are Created Equal

The truth is that not all ecolabels are created equal. Some hardly qualify as ecolabels at all. The best ones directly support and reward on-the-ground change and channel as much money as possible back to the actual producers themselves. (Certifiers of fair-trade, organic, and shade-grown coffee labels, for example, often work directly with grower cooperatives.) Others are "cause-related" marketing efforts that merely fundraise by printing a nonprofit organization's logo and information about its

mission on a product or package in return for a percentage of sales.

Mainstream industry trade groups often counter
ecolabel programs by launching voluntary initiatives of their own. Their names are very compelling
sounding or vaguely worded, to obscure the constituencies behind them. In North America, the
American Forest and Paper Association responded
to the Forest Stewardship Council's (FSC) sustainable forestry ecolabel by establishing its own
Sustainable Forestry Initiative. The FSC is an independent third-party organization founded by a
global constituency of foresters, industry, environmental organizations, biologists, and other stakeholders. In contrast, at its inception, the Sustainable
Forestry Initiative was a voluntary program,
founded and funded by an industry trade group
with less-ambitious standards. Europe also
responded to the FSC with the industry-sponsored
Pan European Forest Certification Council. While
industry-sponsored initiatives such as these can
sometimes result in improvements in best management practices, they are seldom as far-reaching as
those conducted by noninterested third parties
advocating for higher and more appropriate on-the-
ground change. Industry groups are also usually
better funded, and for the consumer these competing labels can create a great deal of confusion.

In response to these discrepancies in real benefits, and as a service to concerned citizens, some
consumer advocate organizations are now closely
studying the ecolabel movement. In other words,
watchdogs watch the watchdogs. This is a good
thing. The Consumers Union launched a Web site
in 2001 to help consumers navigate the increasingly complex web of claims and track records of
various ecolabels.[108] In addition to assessing the
broad range of ecolabels operating in the marketplace, it offers fundamental criteria that ecolabels
should abide by:

- **Clear.** Labels should have well-defined standards that are meaningful and verifiable and
  that support them.
- **Consistent.** Labels with variable standards
  depending on the product can be misleading
  to consumers.
- **Transparent.** Information about organizational
  structure, funding, board of directors, and certification standards must be publicly available.
- **Independent.** Organizations establishing standards and deciding who can use a logo should
  have no ties to users and shouldn't get money
  from them, except for certification fees.
- **Democratic.** All interested parties should be
  heard before standards are adopted.

In a perfect world, there would be no need for
third-party ecolabel organizations. They create
additional layers of bureaucracy and regulation
that can absorb resources. In some cases, product
premiums benefit the foreign certifying organization and middlemen more than the actual producers. In a perfect world, every supplier would define

social and environmental best practices and be remunerated for incorporating those standards into specifications for materials and processing. There are isolated examples of companies doing just that, but they are unfortunately the exception rather than the rule.

In the medium term, however, ecolabels and certification organizations are providing valuable mechanisms to bring producers and consumers together through market-based solutions. How they affect the world of packaging remains to be seen. At least two third-party certification organi-zations (the FSC and the Chlorine-Free Products Association) currently bear a direct impact on packaging materials: one that sets standards for sustainable forestry, and one that monitors chlorine-free pulping practices. Of course, the expanding markets for certified products (particularly organic) will eventually require a shift toward packaging systems that match the environmental standards of sustainable production. In addition to further validating the product histories of goods produced at faraway sites, it could create innovations for other industries.

The Forest Stewardship Council's 10 Principles

1 Meet all applicable laws and FSC principles.

2 Have legally established, long-term forest management rights.

3 Recognize and respect the rights of indigenous peoples.

4 Maintain the economic and social well-being of local communities.

5 Conserve the forests' economic resources.

6 Protect biological diversity.

7 Have a written management plan.

8 Engage in regular monitoring and assessment.

9 Conserve primary forests and well-developed secondary forests.

10 Manage plantations so as to alleviate pressures on natural forests.

Source: www.fscus.org

The Forest Stewardship Council: Certified Wood and the Well-Managed Working Forest

Like food and fiber crops grown according to organic rules, or coffee raised under biologically appropriate levels of shade, wood products certified by the Forest Stewardship Council (FSC) adhere to standards established to promote "well-managed" forests. On a landscape level, FSC emphasizes the protection of biodiversity and native species. Management plans are based on long-term, sustainable yields for a given property. Special care is given to avoiding riparian zones (rivers and streams) and wetland areas and conserving intact primary and secondary forests. Acknowledging industrial forestry's direct effects on the well-being of local communities and indigenous peoples, social concerns must also be addressed. In an effort to accommodate the tremen-

dous demand for wood fiber, managed plantation forests are eligible for certification.

With so much of the world's waste stream comprising wood-based paper, packaging, and construction materials, a dramatic increase in FSC-certified raw materials could have a significant influence on the world's forests. Packaging materials could range from pulp for virgin-wood-based paperboard to lumber for pallet stocks. Percentage-based products—such as paper, particle board, and corrugated that often require a certain amount of virgin fibers for strength—need not contain 100 percent FSC materials to receive the seal. Until 2005 they must contain at least 30 percent FSC content to qualify. After that, the percentage-based minimum increases to 50 percent.

Certifying a sustainably harvested and produced packaging material means hiring third-party monitors to track the entire chain of custody from the forest through the mill or manufacturing plant. Obviously, not every tree felled, board sawn, or vat pulped can be overseen. Instead, exemplary companies, individual foresters, mills, manufacturers, and retailers qualify for certification and agree to adhere to the organization's "principles of stewardship" (see page 93), which include routine monitoring and assessment. A number of organizations work closely with the FSC to certify foresters, producers, and manufacturers under wide-ranging conditions: The Rainforest Alliance's Smart Wood program and Scientific Certification Systems in North America; the Soil Association and SGS Forestry Qualifor in the United

Kingdom; Silva Forest Foundation in Canada; Skal in the Netherlands; and Institut für Marktökologie in Switzerland, among others.

An offshoot of the 1992 United Nations Conference on Environment and Development held in Rio de Janeiro, the FSC burst onto the world scene as a nonprofit, nongovernmental, global organization. Formerly with international headquarters in Oaxaca, Mexico, the main FSC body is now centered in Berlin. While far from perfect, this organization has worked diligently to forge interdisciplinary production standards, build markets, raise awareness, and influence the supply of products from well-managed woodlands. By 2003, the end of its first decade, the FSC had certified nearly 100 million acres on five continents, spanning small community holdings on tropical islands to multimillion-acre tracts in northern boreal forests. North American paper companies that may soon introduce FSC-certified, paper-based packaging materials include Tembec, Norske, and Domtar.

Rival Standards

The popular appeal of a "good wood" seal did not go unnoticed by the global forest products industry. Today, more than 50 voluntary wood certification programs are in place worldwide. Following the establishment of the FSC in 1993, the American Forest and Paper Association launched its own heavily funded North American certification program, the Sustainable Forestry Initiative (SFI). For years the SFI functioned as a voluntary program, with vague standards that primarily hinged on self-monitoring. Many critics likened the lack of outside auditing to letting the fox guard the henhouse. Responding to valid criticisms and the challenge of the FSC's international success, however, the SFI has gradually raised its standards and moved toward certification by noninterested third parties.

There is enough legitimate criticism for all of these programs. While industry-sponsored initiatives have improved and continue to incite change, they have also been guilty of using green labels as a marketing ploy—applying them to status quo rather than to exemplary products. As yet, there appear to be no outright bans on clearcutting, the use of toxic herbicides, or genetically modified tree species. (Even the FSC sanctions clearcutting and herbicides under certain conditions.) Logging within government-owned forests is still permitted, at least partially because in some countries, like Canada, the majority of forestry takes place on public lands. And in an effort to boost supply in the marketplace, a few large companies have been awarded certification based upon the promise of future management rather than proven on-the-ground performance.

Most environmentally minded observers, however, still view the FSC as the leading forest certification organization and the best hope for establishing a worldwide matrix of working forests that balance economic output, biodiversity protection, and the varied interests of human communities. The packaging industry is only beginning to see the immense value in rallying behind these standards.

Alliance for Environmental Innovation: The "Greener" Boxboard Project

When the economy revs up, packaging is among the first industries to respond. Perhaps not surprisingly, North America's capacity for the production of paperboard—the material of boxes and folding cartons used to package all kinds of consumer products from carryout food to cosmetics—grew by 30 percent during the economic boom of the 1990s. Concerned about the impacts of such a massive increase in the volume of wood-based packaging material, the Boston-based Alliance for Environmental Innovation (AEI) released a report entitled "Greener Cartons: A Buyer's Guide to Recycled-Content Paperboard."

Three basic types of paperboard are used in packaging consumer goods: coated recycled board (CRB); solid bleached sulfate (SBS); and coated unbleached kraft (CBK). According to the AEI, when it comes to greener cartons, CRB is the material of choice because it is made from recovered materials with a minimum of 35 percent post-consumer waste. It is available in a wide range of thicknesses, exhibits high-quality printability, is cost-competitive and often cheaper to use, can be printed as fast as other materials, and has a favorable perception among consumers. In addition, it uses valuable post-consumer materials, cuts greenhouse gas emissions, and reduces wastewater discharges, among other benefits. The coat-

ing is typically a combination of clay, latex, and titanium that offers the brightness and vibrant graphics that marketers require. Over the past 20 years, CRB has cost between 25 and 40 percent less per ton than virgin board. This alone should have companies converting to it. Even when using the highest-quality and heaviest-basis weights to compensate, CRB performs well and has cost advantages over standard SBS.

Packaging specifiers can also switch to paperboard with an outer layer of SBS and an inner layer of recycled material with a post-consumer content of between 10 and 35 percent. According to the study, the cost of these virgin/recycled blends ranges between 10 percent less and 9 percent more than conventional SBS.

Information, sources, and options are what most designers need to get started, and AEI paperboard project manager Bruce Hammond recommends that studios keep a regularly updated list of suppliers and product samples and conduct trial print runs for brightness, smoothness, printability, and other factors. The 100% Recycled Paperboard Alliance is a good source of suppliers such as Rock Tenn, Smurfit, Stone, Caraustar, Banner, Cascades, and The Newark Group. Companies and organizations can also use the alliance's Paper Calculator to quantify the environmental benefits (greenhouse gas and wastewater emissions, solid-waste reductions, and tree savings) gained by choosing post-consumer content paper or paperboard for specific projects.

Summit Brewery:
More Palatable Pallets

What do the origins of wood pallets and the quality of beer have in common? Apparently, water. In the summer of 2002, Summit Brewery of Saint Paul, Minnesota, celebrated the introduction of transport pallets made of FSC-certified wood harvested from nearby state and county forestlands.

"Buying FSC-certified pallets encourages forest management practices that protect clean water resources—an essential ingredient in quality beer," says Christopher Siotz, general manager of Summit Brewing. "We especially like the direct connection between well-managed forests in the Mississippi watershed supplying wood for our pallets and protecting the quality of the water we use for our brewing."[109]

Resigned that a century of overcutting and "high grading" (the selective harvesting of only the most marketable trees) have left the state's forests in desperate need of healing, the Minnesota Department of Natural Resources along with Cass and Aitkin counties began looking into the benefits of FSC certification. By 2003, Minnesota had enrolled nearly one million acres in county, state, and private forest lands in FSC programs.

Management plans frequently require the thinning of smaller-diameter, lower-value trees in the short term, in order to restore a healthier, uneven-aged structure to forests. Pallets are the highest value-added product among potential commercial uses for those trees. To get a market-based initiative off the ground, however, potential buyers had to be linked with suppliers. The Community Forestry Resource Center, a project of the Minneapolis-based Institute for Agriculture and Trade Policy, conducted essential research and networking to nudge the market along. Two suppliers (Stewart's Forest Products and Savanna Pallet) quickly stepped in to explore the niche among green businesses seeking transport containers made from regionally supplied, certified materials. For both companies, the chain-of-custody certification (which monitors the entire supply line from the forest to the end user) became a means of expanding their product lines and distinguishing their environmental values. In addition to Summit Brewery, Aveda, the Minnesota-based personal care products manufacturer, agreed to phase in FSC-certified pallets to its distribution fleet.

FSC-Certified Wood Pallets.
Introduced in 2002, FSC-certified pallets are made of materials harvested from county, state, and private lands in Minnesota. Summit Brewery of Saint Paul and Minneapolis-based Aveda are among the first companies using the third-party-certified pallets.

The Chlorine-Free Products Association: Processing Without Chlorine

Just as urgent as packaging's footprint on forests or its contribution to global warming is the ubiquitous use of chlorine in the production of paperboard, certain plastics, and other elements and additives. Organochlorines—including dioxins, furans, polychlorinated biphenyl (PCB), and other compounds associated with chlorine-based pulping, certain plastics production, and waste incineration—are known to cause adverse health effects to the nervous, immune, and reproductive systems of humans and animals.[110] These are among the world's most persistent atmospheric and water contaminants. They travel widely, attaching themselves to fat molecules, moving up the food chain. Both the U.S. Environmental Protection Agency and the Institute of Environmental Health Sciences list dioxin as a known human carcinogen. According to the Worldwatch Institute, the average virgin-paper mill releases 35 tons of organochlorine compounds per day.[111] On a yearly basis, wastewater discharges from paper mills total in the trillions of gallons.[112]

In the early 1990s, European paper mills shifted toward "totally chlorine-free" pulping technologies to drastically reduce toxic emissions by substituting ozone and hydrogen peroxide systems in the bleaching and delignification of virgin-wood fibers. By contrast, most North American mills chose to upgrade to less expensive and less effec-tive "elemental chlorine-free" pulping systems. Depending on the mill and exact processing equipment, elemental chlorine-free bleaching tehnology typically relies on chlorine dioxide as a pulp brightener. This eliminates 90 percent (but not all) of the harmful byproducts.

Of course, paper appears as a major ingredient in the packaging chain, as labels, instructional manuals, fillers, and other elements. Chlorine also shows up in inks, adhesives, and certain plastics. Polyvinyl chloride, or PVC, commonly used for clear clamshell "blister packs" that dominate discount-store merchandising as well as for seldom recycled No. 3 drink bottles, is another environmental packaging villain. PVC is hazardous to manufacture, requiring heavy metal stabilizers and toxic plasticizers to make it usable.[113] In its landmark study, the Tellus Institute reported that PVC production releases more toxicity per ton than any other packaging material, particularly in the form of vinyl chloride monomer and other carcinogenic substances.[114] Experts have long argued that PVC could be immediately replaced by other chlorine-free plastics for just a minimal rise in costs but with invaluable environmental benefits. It remains a seldom recycled plastic on the market today.

A Bright Sign: Certified Chlorine-Free

For over a decade, the Chlorine-Free Products Association (CFPA), based in Algonquin, Illinois, has been building markets for chlorine-free products by certifying papers and other products. CFPA's third-party monitoring system tracks an entire product's history, ensuring that they (1) contain no old-growth timber in virgin-pulp, (2) use no chlorine or chlorine compounds in processing, (3) accurately report post-consumer content and contain a minimum of 20 percent post-consumer waste, and (4) are produced in mills with no pending or current violations.

Huhtamaki Certified Chlorine-Free Molded Pulp

Anyone who has attended a sporting event understands the practicality of the molded pulp carrier. It's that low-slung, egg-carton gray tray that holds two drinks, a hot dog, and fries. Huhtamaki, a Finnish multinational that supplies packaging materials in 34 countries, owns two U.S. plants (formerly Chinette) that manufacture 80 tons of rough-finished molded fiber for fast-food trays. Its sole feedstock, recycled newsprint, is pulped without chlorine—meaning the trays qualify as "processed chlorine-free." "Totally chlorine-free" would require that no chlorine be used on the original newsprint. At present, the paper and collection industries don't have systems to isolate virgin-wood-based papers as they are used and recovered.

In the summer of 2002, Huhtamaki initiated the certification process with the CFPA on its carrier trays sold to restaurants, colleges, and universities. By 2003, the certification was complete, affirming that the carriers are made from old-growth-free,

post-consumer content pulp and processed with no harmful chlorine chemistry in mills that have no environmental permit violations. One of Huhtamaki's future goals is to develop certified direct-food-contact containers such as plates and food dishes. This will require new generations of coatings that are heat tolerant and provide adequate moisture and thermal barriers.

●**Totally chlorine-free (TCF).** Refers to virgin paper made without the use of chlorine or chlorine derivatives. The term cannot be associated with recycled papers as there is no way of tracking how original fibers were bleached.

●**Processed chlorine-free (PCF).** Refers to the processing of recycled pulp with a bleaching process free of chlorine or chlorine compounds. The most commonly used agent is hydrogen peroxide, which breaks down into water and oxygen. Using PCF agents eliminates most of the toxic byproducts of traditional bleaching.

●**Elemental chlorine-free (ECF).** A bleaching process that uses chlorine compounds such as chlorine dioxide to brighten pulp. Modern ECF bleaching agents have significantly lower environmental impacts than the traditional chlorine-gas bleaching method. Some mills rely on ozone and other technologies to further reduce toxic outputs.

The Rise of the Mini-Mill

At the cost of a billion dollars or more, the modern paper mill ranks high among industries in terms of capital intensiveness. In order to drive down unit costs in a climate of overproduction, mills engage in continuous 24-hour production marathons, consuming the energy of small municipalities and the equivalent of 75-acre clearcuts on a daily basis.[115] The two-month supply of wood chips needed to keep one Oregon-based cardboard mill in production, for example, occupies an area 40–50 acres across and 1 foot deep.[116] With such a massive commitment to existing and sometimes outdated infrastructure, few corporations have been willing to invest in the radical upgrades and adjustments necessary to advance production equipment to meet today's environmental and efficiency standards. In the United States, papermaking ranks third in terms of toxic pollution (behind car exhaust and steel production) and fourth in energy intensiveness, yet still produces only 1 ton of paper for every 2–3.5 tons of raw wood materials processed.[117]

Over the past few decades, the concept of the "mini-mill" has often been cited as a preferred alternative to the highly centralized, capital-, energy-, and chemical-intensive manufacturing facilities that increasingly produce the majority of materials we use and consume every day. Taking their name from a steel-industry term, these mini-mill systems, such as those that make paperboard, wall board, building blocks, and other products, are intended to take advantage of local resource bases, both virgin and recovered, while manufacturing products with the surrounding population or nearby industries as a primary market. Part of the appeal of the mini-mill is its relatively low cost of capitalization. With start-up costs under $100 million (sometimes far less than that), it is believed, these mills can be strategically located in different areas and engineered with the long-term flexibility to adapt to new technologies as they evolve. In terms of environmental production standards, mini-mills usually set the bar extremely high compared with conventional industry. They strive for zero effluent and emissions (no water or air pollution), minimal chemical inputs, and extremely high rates of water and energy efficiency.

Ideally, these mills are situated to take particular advantage of underutilized resources that, at least theoretically, offer short-term economic advantages. Agricultural areas are often identified as having high mini-mill potential, where fiber crops can be grown intentionally (such as industrial hemp, kenaf, or flax for both oilseed and fiber) or where agricultural residues (leftover straw from grain, corn, or sugar production) are undervalued and could boost the regional economy. The industrial rice-growing area and highly urbanized region of the Sacramento Valley, in California, has been the site of a few efforts to locate a mini-mill that could process rice straw and recycled office paper into paper products for Northern California consumption. (To date, efforts have fallen short, though there are a few companies producing building materials from the straw.) Cargill Dow's Blair, Nebraska, plant was strategically located to manufacture biodegradable plastics from the Corn Belt's oversupply of corn starch, though it can hardly be classed as a mini-mill. Attempts have been brewing to build a pulp mill using the fast-growing fiber crop kenaf as a primary feedstock in Texas and other areas of the South for some time. Canada seems to be leading North America in experimenting with and promoting industries using nonwood fibers such as flax, wheat straw, and industrial hemp.

Breaking into existing markets by infusing a commodity like cardboard or plastic with an ecological-added value, however, has proven a formidable challenge. Premiums for environmentally preferable cardboard, wallboard, and the like are marginal at best and, without adequate profits, will fail to attract necessary private sector involvement. Thus the operative question lies in qualifying the optimum size and configuration of "mini." Regardless of the industry, these mills must achieve an appropriate scale and distribution network to bring products to market at a competitive price while generating a return on investment.

With an emphasis on recycled rather than virgin materials and on high rates of resource efficiency, however, mini-mills could ultimately set themselves up as industry's low-cost producers. The choice of an existing "brownfield" site where a commercial or industrial facility was previously located can prevent sprawl and habitat degradation, and reduce transportation-related impacts.[118] Rather than consuming quality potable water sources, mini-mills can be designed to consume cleaned sewage effluent as a valuable industrial input.

Whether technologies, infrastructures, and political support will align to make resource recovery efficient and affordable remains to be seen. The tale of the Bronx Community Paper Corporation's decade-long attempt to build a mill that would reprocess New York City's vast wastepaper resources serves as a poignant case. Designed as a state-of-the-art, zero-effluent facility at an abandonded railroad yard in South Bronx, the project ultimately failed due to a host of factors, including the costs of union labor, international market forces that offered marginally higher returns across the globe, and basic human avarice. The lessons learned from the project are detailed in the book *Bronx Ecology: Blueprint for a New Environmentalism* by Allen Hershkowitz, the Natural Resources Defense Council's senior scientist who spearheaded the project. Despite the obstacles, Hershkowitz argues that we all must work together to make regionally oriented industrial ecology projects succeed.

Durango-McKinley: Leading-Edge Linerboard

Considering the conventional requirements of abundant water supplies and forest resources, the desert Southwest might seem an unlikely place to site an ultraefficient paper mill. Or perhaps the limitations of water, energy, and resources in the desert would inspire innovation by necessity. Durango-McKinley Paper, a subsidiary of Corporación Durango, is a zero-effluent mini-mill, set in the desert of west-central New Mexico. Built in the mid-1990s, Durango-McKinley relies on the waste streams of its neighboring states—Colorado, Arizona, Utah, Oklahoma, and west Texas—for its raw materials. Arriving in half-ton bales, old corrugated containers—office paper, linerboard, and other post-consumer fibers—are cleaned, sorted, and prepared in a five-stage process. Fiber recovery is surprisingly productive: only 6 percent of the fibers are lost as sludge during reprocessing. The remaining quality fibers are then recycled into lightweight linerboard through North America's first closed-loop water system.

According to Durango-McKinley customer service manager Steve Underwood, the mini-mill technology uses just 1 gallon of water for every 8 gallons used by conventional mega-mills, slashing water consumption by nearly 90 percent. "An equivalent mill built beside a river would easily use 1.2 million gallons of water to produce our daily output of 600 tons of materials. We use 144,000 gallons of fresh water per day," Underwood explained.[119] That water (pumped from an aquifer for energy production at an adjacent coal-fired plant) is needed to run the paper machine, but it is also recycled again and again. The only losses occur through evaporation, moisture content in the paper, and the "press cakes" that are currently being recycled as an off-site soil amendment.

Energy efficiency is another key component of the Durango-McKinley system. Using up-to-date, asynchronous, low-horse-power machinery allows the company to minimize the amount of energy needed per ton of paper. At its inception, the mill was strategically located next to a coal-fired generation plant that serves as a nearby energy source and allows the mill to take advantage of the plant's steam byproducts to dry the paper. Throughout that steam-drying process, water is condensed and recaptured, then sent back to the power plant for reuse. Durango-McKinley is also investigating the feasibility of using solar, wind, or other forms of renewable energy to meet a significant portion of its energy needs.

Recycled pulp has remained competitive globally with virgin fibers since the late 1990s. In fact, because of their longer fibers, old corrugated cartons produced in the United States are highly desirable and often shipped to the Far East, where they are used to fortify straw, bamboo, and other fibers in corrugated production. Durango-McKinley's annual output is 200,000 tons, with products sold regionally to converters on the West Coast. Similar mills are located in Solvay, New York, and Liberty, Minnesota, though their water efficiency and discharge rates are not as low as Durango-McKinley's, according to Underwood.

With its sophisticated water reclamation plant and zero liquid discharge, Durango-McKinley should point the way toward new standards for small-scale regional paper mills throughout North America.

Zero-Effluent Mini-Mill. Durango-McKinley's linerboard facility in New Mexico is a testament to mini-mill technology. The mill relies only on post-consumer waste paper as its raw material and consumes just a fraction of the water used by conventional paper mills.

Regale:
21st-Century Egg Carton

In the mid-1990s, Regale founder Greg Gale embarked on the seemingly simple mission to design a wine-box partition that would make label scuff a thing of the past. Twenty million dollars and a convention-defying plunge into the world of molded-fiber technology later, Gale and about a dozen employees at his start-up company based in Napa, California, are poised to incite a quiet revolution in the packaging industry.

Gale began his packaging career in the late 1970s making wooden wine boxes. In 1986 he shifted to corrugated containers. Even as an accomplished designer of high-end packages with a patent to his credit for a perforated wine case that could be quickly divided into two six-packs, he was frustrated with the limitations of corrugated. "There are only so many ways you can fold a box," he explains.[120] Then one day the malleable, three-dimensional nature of egg-carton technology inspired him as a potential solution to label scuff. Rigid cardboard dividers regularly rub the ink off of labels as bottles shift around during transport, rendering them unsalable. Gale felt a contoured package could remedy the problem.

"The whole thing started by a personal error," Gale explains. With absolutely no knowledge of the manufacturing process for conventional molded-fiber egg-carton technology, he set out to accomplish what most industry insiders considered insane, if not impossible. "We soon got so deep into a jungle that we just had to keep moving forward to find our way out," he says.

What Gale quickly realized was that the conventional method of creating tooling for a molded-fiber package was both time-consuming and expensive. Known commonly in the trade as "barriers to entry," a molded-fiber package could take months to prototype and hundreds of thousands of dollars to produce. Up to that point, these barriers had limited molded fiber to a narrow niche of the packaging market. Fortunately for Gale, timing was on his side. Modern computer technology had finally caught up with the 110-year-old egg-carton material, allowing an entrepreneurially minded outsider to work beyond the confines of the conventional mold.

Gale turned to rapid prototype technology, an innovation of the University of Texas, typically used to make preproduction prototypes and custom, one-off parts for the automobile, aircraft, aerospace, and other similar industries. The system combines industrially aided computer engineering with laser technology and what Gale describes as "a bit of industrial magic." First, a fabric-like, three-dimensional realization of an item is drafted using a CAD (computer-aided design) program. The design is then electronically transferred to a DTM Sinterstation Vanguard 2500 Plus prototyper, a $400,000 off-the-shelf machine not much larger than a commercial copier. A laser-guided crafting process then begins, building a model, top to bottom, layer by layer, out of a polymer powder. Within 48 hours, the excess material is chopped away from a mound of food-grade powder (which Gale has been known to taste), and a tactile prototype emerges that can be analyzed, adjusted, and tweaked accordingly. Once a final design is settled on, the same computer design and prototype machinery can be used to create the male and female molds required to make molded fiber packages on the assembly line. This replaces the heavy metal tools typically cast for such manufacturing, and transforms the rapid prototype machine from an exclusive producer of custom items to a technology of mass production.

"Suddenly the barriers to entry for molded-fiber technology shrink to a matter of days and thousands of dollars. We are able to serve companies large and small and save them a significant amount of money," says Gale. According to Paul Russell, director of enterprise packaging for Hewlett-Packard, Regale's unique manufacturing technology presents the opportunity to develop cost-effective alternatives to polystyrene and other foam cushioning materials. These are key concerns for companies that need to adhere to increasingly enforced take-back laws that have been adopted in more than 30 countries.

Regale's most radical innovation takes place on the assembly line. Using vacuum and hot compressed air to dry the molded-fiber material while it is still inside the mold, Regale is now able to create shapes up to 12 inches tall. The traditional drying process only permitted a very shallow geometry, hence the limitation to egg cartons, apple trays, and other such applications. "We're now able to create

shapes that were never available to this medium," says Gale, "and today these are typically made from foam."

Gale shows off the fruits of the company's various R&D efforts to date: a wine-case insert that accommodates various bottle sizes and serves as a shell for two bottles or a tray for four: a load-bearing cushioning corner system called the "Shock Wave"; a free-form shoe container; a Miro-esque egg carton tray that replaces bubble wrap; a champagne flute divider designed to eliminate an ergonomically

Space-Age Molded Pulp.
California-based Regale has spent nearly a decade developing the technology to use molded pulp made from recycled papers and agricultural residues to service a wide range of packaging needs.

unsafe repetitive task. A few of the prototypes are hung like art objects on Regale's white-walled, high-ceilinged headquarters.

The adjoining manufacturing facility, an 18,000-square-foot warehouse, is the pilot plant for what Regale hopes will become hundreds of "township factories" across the country and the world. In one area stands a shiny stainless vat capable of pulping 31 tons of post-consumer waste paper and old corrugated containers per day. In another are a number of hinged robotic machines that dip the pallet-sized molds into the fibrous goop (99 percent water, 1 percent fiber) before lifting them to an innovative drying mechanism. According to Gale, the manufacturing process has been designed as a closed-loop system that recovers 99.7 percent of its waste water. Regale engineers have also reduced by 40 percent the amount of heat needed to process materials and have increased by a magnitude of hours the speed with which molds can be switched. The only inputs are shredded recycled fibers, water, and considerable amounts of energy. (A typical Regale mini-mill consumes the equivalent electricity budget of 3,000 households, considered efficient compared to the conventional paper industry.) Agricultural fibers, including rice husks, chicken feathers, and fast-growing kenaf have been pulped in collaboration with U.S. Department of Agriculture researchers in nearby Albany, California.

"These mini-mills will be small, athletic, and community oriented," says Gale, waxing optimistically about Regale's grand global plan. After years of hard work, his company has finally assembled the business models and stakeholder alliances needed to launch the trademarked Regale System. The manufacturing module will comprise fiber molding machines, compressors, vacuum pumps, and other elements made by Mitsui Engineering and Shipbuilding. Amcor Sunclipse, an Australian paper conglomerate, is coordinating manufacturing agreements. Ideally, these mini-mills will be located close to manufacturing centers that also have ample power generation to accommodate the system's three 800 horsepower compressors. Raw materials will come from the regional waste stream.

Despite these accomplishments in technology and development, the company still faces a significant hurdle. The first of Regale's planned manufacturing facilities has yet to be established. Although companies such as Adidas, Hewlett-Packard, Libbey Glass, Chalone Winery, and Harry and David have sourced packaging prototypes out of Regale's pilot plant in Napa, California, the alternative packaging start-up has been unable to successfully launch a production factory. Assuming that adequate funding materializes and other variables align, potential sites that have been mentioned include Alameda, California, El Paso, Texas, Memphis, Tennessee, and locations in Asia.

Perhaps because of these economic realities, it's hard to find a trace of green evangelism in the Regale pitch. "Performance is the key to this new packaging system," says Gale. "We will be able to provide a better product at less cost, and that's an

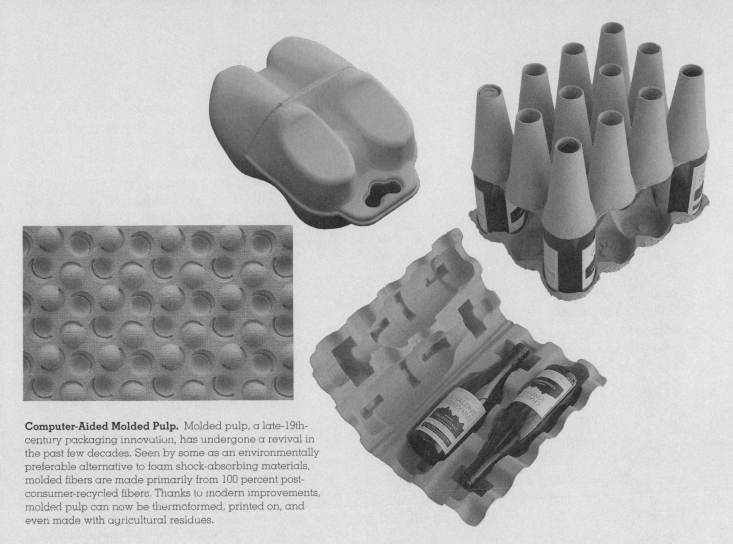

Computer-Aided Molded Pulp. Molded pulp, a late-19th-century packaging innovation, has undergone a revival in the past few decades. Seen by some as an environmentally preferable alternative to foam shock-absorbing materials, molded fibers are made primarily from 100 percent post-consumer-recycled fibers. Thanks to modern improvements, molded pulp can now be thermoformed, printed on, and even made with agricultural residues.

easy sell inside a corporation. The added values are to the environment, the community, and the chance to do away with heinous assembly-line tasks by creating new packaging solutions."

Looking back on his adventure, Gale is still amazed by the possibilities of this new system. While manufacturing remains an integral component of the Regale business plan, he insists that design will always be the driving force. "Packaging is primarily a logistical vehicle," he says, "and you don't need a 747 to travel a block. People are finally becoming aware of all the excess and they're complaining about it. Our job as designers is minimization, minimization, minimization. Hypothetically, the ultimate package would be a force field. It protects the article and you can't even see it."

The Carbohydrate Economy: On the Trail of Bioplastics

Making plastic packaging from plant materials that can safely and naturally decompose is a curiously seductive concept. To appreciate the logic, one only has to envision reprocessing or composting (into carbon dioxide and water) all the food and beverage packaging associated with a single sporting event of, say, 40,000 people. And with municipalities launching programs to collect and compost household food waste, interest in degradable plastics is on the rise. Some European countries have already banned organic matter from landfills. A much smaller number of U.S. cities and counties, including San Francisco, are collecting household organic wastes in separate curbside containers, though municipal composting is developing far more slowly than advocates had hoped. In mid-2002, Taiwan took steps to ban plastic shopping bags and single-use disposable packaging and tableware. Since that time, a number of municipal and regional initiatives have been made to ban disposable take-out packaging and plastic bags, or what is increasingly referred to as "white pollution."

The Dawning of Bioplastics

The modern pursuit of bioplastics and biofuels is at least 80 years old, driven in part by the desire to discover industrial applications for ever-increasing agricultural surpluses. Back in the days of Bakelite and the Great Depression, assembly-line pioneer Henry Ford became one of the founding proponents of the Chemurgy movement, an effort to reverse rural poverty by creating new markets and uses for field crops. By the 1940s, Ford Motor Company researchers succeeded at manufacturing lightweight exterior car panels from the "annual produce of the fields," such as soybeans and industrial hemp, and fueling automobiles with ethanol. Wooden crates containing Louisiana Spanish moss, an upholstery stuffing, were also reportedly disassembled and installed as floor-board materials on early Ford cars. With the rise of cheap fossil fuels and petroleum-based plastics in the post–World War II era, however, the Chemurgist dream faded back into the fields. Now, following a 50-year hiatus, there has been a revival of biobased materials. Nearly all major automotive manufacturers have experimented with composites made from agricultural crop residues like wheat straw, bagasse (sugar cane), and coconut husks. Paper and construction material producers have also worked to find ways of incorporating the tens of millions of tons of underutilized wheat and rice straw, rye grass, and other annual crop byproducts in corrugated, fiber board, and other pressed and molded products. And for at least two decades, companies, government researchers, and others have been developing the technology and markets for a biobased plastics industry.

Starch peanuts and biodegradable bags are probably the most widely distributed agro-synthetic plastics in the mainstream today, although the terrain is rapidly changing. A handful of the world's most powerful corporations have entered the bioplastic packaging market, including DuPont, Cargill Dow, BASF, Eastman Chemical, Proctor and Gamble, Novamont, Zenica ICI, and EarthShell (a publicly traded corporation partially founded by the brother of infamous Saudi investor and arms dealer Adnan Khashoggi). Japan is one of the more active players in the bioplastic movement. In 2002, Mitsubishi Plastics introduced a vegetable-starch-based shock-resistant packaging in Sony Walkman portable headphone sets. That same year, Toyota's concept cars featured interiors detailed with sweet-potato bioplastic as well as trims made from bamboo and flax.[121] And Mitsubishi's polyester carbonate material is now being used as a hardshell yet degradable body material for Sony consumer electronic goods.[122]

Always hunting for opportunities to convert agricultural commodities into value-added products, researchers at the U.S. Department of Agriculture have been promoting the development of "biorefineries" as part of a national renewable resource strategy. These processing mills could greatly expand our ability to convert excess starches and cellulose into a wide strata of products, including food additives, solvents, fuel, various plastics, fabrics, and other goods. USDA scientists at the Albany, California, research lab, who frequently collaborate with private industry on biobased packaging development, have already produced edible films and containers made from pressed or extruded excess fruit and vegetable pulp. Although the ultimate packaging applications remain in question, these veggie and fruit wraps have fielded a considerable amount of commercial interest.

In the United States, bioplastic engineering efforts fall into three primary categories: converting plant starches and sugars into plastics; producing plastic inside microorganisms via fermentation; and genetically modifying crops such as corn and rapeseed so that they actually *grow plastic*. All of these approaches appear to be in various stages of development and commercialization, as outlined below:

● **Polylactic acid.** Leading the charge is the joint-venture by Cargill Dow, which constructed a $300 million plant in Blair, Nebraska, in the late 1990s to refine corn syrup into polylactic acid (PLA) resins, marketed under the brand name NatureWorks (see p. 115). Among the more energy efficient of the typically energy-intensive biobased resins, PLA can be synthesized into both rigid and flexible materials, and is currently used in blow-molded deli trays as well as in various film applications.

● **Isosorbide.** Another product derived from corn sugars, isosorbide is an up-and-coming biodegradable polymer with excellent optical clarity and the ability to make plastics stiffer and allow them to be "hot-filled." Predominantly used by the pharamceutical and chemical industries, a number of corporations are pursuing technologies and patents to make isosorbide production much cheaper (Archer Daniels Midland, Celanese, and DuPont, to name a few). One potential packaging application would be adding isosorbide to PET (whose acronym would then be PEIT), which reduces by 25 percent the amount of material needed to produce a beverage container.

● **Starch and limestone composites.** After a prolonged start-up phase that included a few partnership turnovers, EarthShell eventually joined forces with DuPont to make biodegradable sandwich "clamshells," plates, and other single-use containers. EarthShell blends starches derived from french-fry potato cut-offs or wheat gluten residues in a slurry of recycled paper fibers, limestone, and other fillers. The resulting gooey batter is cooked and hydraulically pressed, yielding a hybrid material somewhere between paper and foam. A biodegradable coating adds a vapor barrier. The packages are said to thoroughly compost in four to six months. Initially, EarthShell set its sights on supplying McDonald's with hamburger containers. After succeeding in producing a suitable clamshell box, however, the company struggled with the complexities of scaling up its manufacturing to meet McDonald's needs. EarthShell containers received high-profile attention at both the Sidney and the Salt Lake City Olympic Games but have yet to take the fast-food nation by storm. Higher costs are at least one significant factor. Another key difficulty has been the need to develop a whole new generation of equipment that can "bake" their biobased foams. Advocates are hoping that a less ambitious, more decentralized marketing strategy might save this 12-year-old, $300 million venture.[123]

Apack, a German manufacturer, also markets biodegradable starch and limestone food contact containers that are cooked, molded, and coated with a vapor barrier. The company guarantees that 99.7 percent of the tray will biodegrade in a compost pile within six weeks.

● **Plastic-producing bacteria.** On another front, bacteria are being use to turn sugars and acids into polyhydroxyalkanoate pellets that can be converted into bottles and other products. In fact, numerous common microorganisms can process sugars into polypropylene-like polymers. Wella Balsam and The Body Shop introduced these bioplastic shampoo bottles to Europe for a time in the 1990s, despite extremely high costs. For many years, Monsanto attempted to genetically engineer those enzymes into canola plants. This approach could not have been more literal—redesigning a single plant to produce two high-yield crops: oil seed and bioplastic pellets. Although genetic engineers actually succeeded in modifying crops with plastic-producing enzymes inside them, Mother Nature apparently had certain limitations. It seems the opaque plastic beads turned the leaves pale, inhibiting plant growth. Monsanto abandoned the effort when profitability failed to materialize. The Boston-based firm Metabolix has since picked up the patents with hopes of using polyhydroxyalkanoate primarily for medical applications. Cost-competitive substitutes for polyethylene could one day come from this family of bioplastics.

The Cornification of Packaging

On the surface, these and other bioplastics seem to provide a solution to the dilemma of petroleum-based plastic containers. According to one expert, 80 million tons of crude oil are consumed each year in the production of plastics in the United States alone, with known reserves predicted to dry up within 80 years. (Most of that fossil fuel is expended in energy generation, however; only a few percent actually become polymers.) Bioplastics also hold out the promise of remedying the paradox of plastic and foam packages outlasting the products they protect by hundreds of years.

For a more complete picture of bioplastics, you must be willing to dig a little deeper. In the United States, a revolution in bioplastics would be predicated, at least in the short term, on the perpetuation of corn and soybean production, an industrial system that has converted the ecosystems of entire midwestern counties to just a single crop. Corn is cultivated over a 125,000-square-mile area in the United States, despite the fact that it costs farmers about one-third more to grow than it earns on the world market. In the United States, transgenic corn varieties engineered with herbicide tolerance as well as the insecticidal bacteria *Baccillus thuringensis* now account for 40 percent of the annual corn crop. This is despite the fact that some studies show herbicide-tolerant genetically modified corn, soybeans, and other crops have actually triggered a long-term increase, rather than a decrease, in chemical use.[124] Genetically engineered corn varieties have contaminated a substantial portion of the U.S. seed supply (as have genetically modified soybean and canola varieties), and scientists are concerned that Mexico's original land-race maize varieties are now at severe risk of irreversible genetic contamination.[125] Perhaps most significant is the vast amount of habitat that has been lost to the production of a single crop used primarily as an animal feed and processed food additive. Writing about corn in an op-ed to the *New York Times*, acclaimed food and agriculture journalist Michael Pollan reported that

> Modern corn hybrids are the greediest of plants, demanding more nitrogen fertilizer than any other crop. Corn requires more pesticide than any other food crop. Runoff from these chemicals finds its way into the groundwater, and, in the Midwestern corn belt, into the Mississippi River, which carries it to the Gulf of Mexico, where it has already killed off marine life in a 12,000 square mile area. . . . America's corn crop might look like a sustainable, solar-powered system for producing food, but it is

actually a huge, inefficient, polluting machine that guzzles fossil fuel—a half a gallon of it for every bushel.[126]

Although corn might be a renewable resource, it is at present not a sustainable one. Sure, it can be grown every year, but over what scale and at what long-term costs? Then there is the question of how much corn would actually be needed to supply the massive industrial quantities modern packaging demand. According to Tillman Gerngross, a professor of engineering at Dartmouth University and bioplastic researcher, nearly 20 million acres of crops—over one-third of the present corn crop—would be required to provide the 30 million tons of plastic polymers consumed in the United States every year.[127] Granted, there is the future possibility that bioplastics will eventually be made not of processed corn oil but from the stover, or plant stalks that typically rot in the fields after harvest. Corn stover could potentially be separated into a variety of biorefinery products, such as cellulose for plastic feed stock, lignins to fuel the fermentation process, and ethanol for fuels. Taking this one step further, those bioplastics could theoretically be reprocessed into new packages or returned to fields in the form of compost—or it could, that is, with adequate collection systems.

Ideally, 21st-century agriculture will change radically from how it is today. In a more sustainable future, monocultures of multi-thousand-acre corn fields will give way to polycultures of more diverse food and fiber crops bordered by interconnected corridors of wilder habitat. Dependence on synthetic fertilizers and other off-farm pesticides will be replaced by systems that emphasize crop rotations that break pest cycles and regenerate soil productivity without the need for off-farm synthetic substances. Biobased products that originate on the farm will be made either from high-yielding, intentionally grown fiber crops or from the residues of food and seed crops such as corn stover, straw, cane, wheat, sugar beets, potatoes, or grass seed. Perhaps, adhering to the biomimicry model, even restored grasslands could one day be judicially harvested to yield a source of native cellulose such as switchgrass.

Energy Efficiency: Bioplastics' Achilles Heel?

Reporting in an article in *Scientific American* magazine, Tillman Gerngross and Steven Slater conducted a thorough study into the energy consumption of corn- and oil-based plastics. They concluded that, contrary to what they expected to find, making bioplastics from corn can (depending on the process) consume many times more energy than producing it from oil. In addition to the actual farming of corn outlined by Pollan previously, extracting oils from corn, say Gerngross and Slater, is an energy-intensive endeavor. Only one present model, the production of starch-based polylactic acid bioplastics being pioneered by Cargill Dow, was found to consume 20–50 percent less fossil fuels to process than making plastics from oil.[128] "It is impossible to argue that plastic grown in corn and extracted with energy from fossil fuels would conserve fossil resources," they concluded.[129]

Gerngross and Slater didn't rule out that developments in technologies could drastically reverse this situation, or that wheat, beets, or other crops easier to process than corn could provide options that are less energy-intensive. At the time of their study, however, the authors determined that it was the source of energy, not the feedstock, that needed greening up the most. "When you look at the global carbon flux," Gerngross said in a later interview, "the amount going to produce plastic resins is a mere 2 percent of the total. The other 98 percent of fossil carbon is used to produce energy."[130] In their article, the authors concluded, "Interestingly, it was switching to a plant-based energy source— not using plants as a raw material—that generated the primary environmental benefit. . . . It appears that both emissions and the depletion of fossil resources would be abated by continuing to make plastics from oil while substituting renewable biomass as the fuel."[131]

It must be said that all life-cycle studies carry biases and capture only a snapshot in time. Yet Gerngross and Slater's point is well taken. How significant are the benefits of using renewable raw materials if they are dwarfed by the climate-altering impacts of coal-fired plants fueling energy-intensive manufacturing processes? Renewable energy is slowly surfacing as an urgent concern in the upper midwestern Corn Belt in recent years, with many constituencies advocating wind farms as a viable alternative. Such a large-scale shift from carbon-based to wind power and other renewable forms of energy, however, will require a major infrastructure investment and overhaul. It will also demand nothing less than a mini-revolution to move from centralized to more decentralized energy grids. Finally, the report tugs at the deeper question—what should be done with our increasingly limited fossil-fuel resources?

Costs and Opportunities

Numerous short-term challenges lie ahead for bioplastics, not the least of which remains cost. Given current technologies and economic complexities, competing commercially with paper, polyethylene, polypropylene, and polystyrene is difficult to impossible. Initial hopes that increasing levels of municipal composting, the avoidance of advance disposal taxes, and the marketability of "green" packaging would boost the profitability of bioplastics have failed to pan out. The rare exception has been in some film markets, where low costs of disposal have been a benefit. But in North America, the infrastructure for sorting and composting organic waste is developing at a snail's pace. And, more often than not, the perceived value of being "green" is trumped by bottom-line costs.[132]

Other present limitations such as water solubility and low heat thresholds—the same factors that make these plastics compostable—present obstacles as well as opportunities. Because many of these bioplastics exhibit different properties, intense research is now focusing on the blending of polymers to produce new ranges of performance and profitability. Within a few years, it is hoped, a new age of plant-based coatings, water barriers, plastic softeners, and adhesives will arrive. Used in combination with either biobased or single-material petroleum-based resins, these degradable additives could potentially replace certain heavy metals, phthalate plasticizers, and other so-called bad actors now widely applied today. That, in turn, could increase the ability to recover and reprocess packaging. Such potential innovations have led insiders to deem bioplastics an essential future "helper technology."

Conclusion

Bioplastics will undoubtedly play an increasing role in industry as part of a larger shift toward more cyclical materials production and recovery. But they may not be the silver bullet many are hoping for. Rather than changing the core of our convenience-oriented society by offering deep systemic solutions, bioplastics seem to offer a plant-based "techno-fix" to our existing consumption habits. In no uncertain terms, a shift to bioplastics will be tied to our addiction to crop surpluses and to our rampant consumption of single-use packages. Yet this begs a further, equally valid question. How could there possibly be a single silver bullet to the packaging dilemma?

Coming to grips with the complex world of bioplastic packaging requires addressing a wide range of issues. What are the agricultural impacts of growing crops to provide the feedstock, including an increase in the use of genetically modified crops? What can be done about the significant amounts of sludge and water contaminants that are byproducts of microbial fermentation? Will greenhouse gases increase as a result of compostable plastics because more energy is needed to grow and process them? Can the inks, glues, barriers, and coatings that are part of these packages be biodegradable as well? How feasible or necessary will it be to create separate waste streams for the collection and reprocessing of synthetic and bioplastics? How will uneven climatic conditions—such as heat and humidity that can speed up or inhibit decomposition—affect the performance of these packages? Can value-added manufacturing be done on a small cooperative scale, or only by major corporations with massive investments?

The age of bioplastics is upon us. Whether it can solve the packaging crisis remains in question.

Cargill Dow: The Corntainer

Amid the corn fields of Nebraska, two multinational titans have joined forces to address one of the ironies of modern consumerism: using petroleum-based materials with centuries-long afterlives to package products that are consumed in a matter of weeks or months. By late 2003, Minnesota-based Cargill Dow had invested three-quarters of a billion dollars in its effort to bring corn starch-based NatureWorks bioplastics to market. That investment had been supplemented with direct and indirect government investments as well: a matching grant from the Department of Energy to explore the feasibility of using stover, or corn stalks, as both a raw material and an energy source; and annual farm bill subsidies that keep upper Midwest farmers growing corn surpluses in the face of plummeting world grain prices. Even with this eye-popping capital output, Cargill Dow still seems to be at the start-up phase of this venture, because present technologies remain far from becoming fully commercialized or developed.

The process of making polylactic acid (PLA) bioplastics begins in a wet mill, as does the manufacture of corn-syrup-based soft drinks. The starches are removed from corn kernels in large cyclindrical vats and later undergo enzyme hydrolysis to yield dextrose. Microbes ferment the dextrose into lactic acid. A further processing stage produces a specifically modified reactive lactide monomer from which longer chains of polymer resins can be produced and later melted, spun, or molded into films, fibers, or thermoforms. Rather than producing finished packaging materials, Cargill Dow sells these biobased resins to fabricators who use them to make molded plastic shells, clear films, containers, disposable wipes, blankets, and bedding fillers. To date, commercial interest has been strongest in Europe and Japan, with fewer U.S. companies lining up to pay the variable premiums that these degradable plastics command. Among Cargill Dow's early North American clients is Wild Oats, an upscale natural foods retailer that purchases blow-molded deli trays made from corn-based plastics.

The afterlife of a PLA container can take a few avenues. The resins can be reprocessed with a relatively high degree of efficiency. They can also be safely incinerated, depending, of course, on the glues, dyes, and any other elements used. Under optimal conditions—surrounded by the heat, moisture, and oxygen found in a municipal composting facility—NatureWorks' corn-based plastics are designed to break down in seven weeks. While this offers a potent antidote for the litter pandemic, the rapid decomposition rate also currently limits PLA's packaging applications. At least for the time being, PLA-plastic doesn't provide a high-quality, long-term moisture barrier. A second limitation is the material's moderately low melt temperature, which apparently can be raised somewhat with additives like talc.

These shortcomings, however, could eventually turn out to be strategic advantages. Coatings and treatments are often one of the barriers that stand between a package made from various comingled plastic materials and recyclability. Using a PLA-based coating that safely decomposes could potentially allow a plastic container to be recycled or a paper-based product to be composted. Perhaps even more significant, with enough research and development, whole plastic packaging systems may one day be replaced altogether.

The Carbon Factor

The move toward bioplastics is in part an attempt to address increasingly scarce fossil fuel resources and unpredictable climate change. So far, life-cycle assessments indicate that PLA plastics outperform their conventional petroleum-based counterparts on a number of levels. The manufacturing process itself, Cargill Dow claims, is 25–40 percent more fossil-fuel efficient than the PET process. There is also the issue of carbon sequestration. Whereas corn crops are living and growing, carbon dioxide is absorbed from the atmosphere and stored in the plant itself—a net gain. Once converted to plastics, however, a number of things can happen: the carbon that the corn soaked in can be (1) transferred into another product via recycling (closed-loop); (2) composted and returned to the atmosphere (carbon neutral); or (3) converted to methane gas as a result of anaerobic landfill conditions (a considerably higher form of greenhouse gas emission, and an undesirable option).

Cornbelt Concerns

Another salient issue is the landscape-level repercussions of using corn directly as a raw material for plastics rather than as a feed for livestock or as a starch and sweetener for processed foods. Approximately 10 percent of the current U.S. corn crop is now surplus. At full capacity, the Cargill Dow Nebraska plant would consume a mere fraction of that: 0.2 percent of the total U.S. corn crop based on year 2000 yields, accounting for just 0.0001 percent of all plastic made from petroleum. With long-term success, however, the need for more raw materials could eventually compete with the demand for food and feed corn. This in turn could drive either a greater intensification of industrial corn production or a radical shift away from our present corn-intensive diet. (While successfully boosting yields, intensive "green revolution" agriculture has often come at considerable environmental expense, such as heightened fertilizer, pesticide, and herbicide loads, soil erosion, energy-intensive mechanization, nutrient leaching, habitat destruction, and the unraveling of rural communities.)

Agricultural Residues: The Next Frontier

Here, the tale of the corntainer takes an interesting twist. To its credit, Cargill Dow has been using life-cycle analysis to set goals and monitor results as well as to map out improvement strategies. Because life-cycle studies have revealed the impacts of the many forms of corn farming (i.e., conventional, no-till, and organic) as well as the potential effects of intensifying corn production, Cargill Dow has been exploring the possibilities of moving beyond corn kernels for its primary feedstock. One possibility would be to use corn stover, which is sometimes tilled back into the soil for organic matter or left to rot. The stover itself is composed mostly of cellulose fibers bound together by lignins. Separated out, it is thought that the lignin can be used to help generate energy for the processing of the cellulose into plastics. This same method could be applied to other agricultural residues—from wheat and rice straw to sugar cane and potentially even native grasses, such as switchgrass.

The Way Ahead

Whether Cargill Dow can create packaging products that help to preserve fossil resources and reverse the devastating trends of conventional agriculture remains to be seen. Given the company's considerable research and investment, it is unlikely that PLA will be a "flash in the pan." Ultimately, the polylactic acid corntainer we know today may just become just one of many building blocks of future bioplastic packaging applications.

"They've already proven that they can make premium-application, disposable-quality products directly competitive within certain tolerances," says Carl Rabago, an environmental analyst formerly with Cargill Dow. "Projections don't bode

Corn-Based Plastics. Containers made in part from corn starch are one of the leading sources of bioplastics. They are designed to decompose in approximately two months under optimal composting conditions. At present, higher costs have limited the widespread use of biodegradable plastics. While made from surplus crops, the ultimate sustainability of these plastics is also related to the impacts of industrial agriculture.

well for petroleum-based plastics, and you can make a lot of other molecules from lactic acid. But as with many things—renewable energy, for instance—widespread change is dependent upon rational markets. We need the involvement of lots of other people. More rapid commercialization will bring more capital to the markets, which in turn can help to solve problems."[133]

The Global Revival of Local Economies

What of the consumer's role in packaging? As purchasers of convenience-oriented, intensively bundled, landfill-bound packs, how complicit are the citizens of industrial nations in the overpackaging dilemma? Poll after poll demonstrates that majorities in most countries rank environmental problems among our top challeneges in the 21st century. Yet we continue to purchase bottled water and produce, electronic goods and household appliances, clothing and furniture, and the stuff of daily life from thousands of miles away from home. This is not a condemnation of foreign trade or packaged goods. As we stated at the outset, we are traders by our nature. But we must acknowledge the consumer's role and enormous potential for change in the global marketplace.

Going Local: In Sight, In Mind

In *The Spell of the Sensuous: Perception and Language in a More Than Human World*, author David Abrams writes: "It is only at the scale of our direct, sensory interactions with the land around us that we can appropriately notice and respond to the immediate needs of the living world."[134] Sensory interactions such as the purchase of newly harvested foods from a farmers' market, the enjoyment of a coffee or dinner at one's favorite cafe or restaurant, the support of a local vendor or artisan, or the making of a meal from local ingredients all set in motion the establishment of known relationships. At best, these patterned exchanges can be motivated by our intentions to support a certain kind of world. They can also directly affect how far goods travel and, in some cases, the extent to which they need to be packaged.

Consider our daily coffee habitat, a ritual that consumes upward of 100 million throwaway cups, sleeves, and lids in a single day in the United States alone. A joint study prepared by the Alliance for Environmental Innovation and Seattle-based Starbucks revealed remarkable economic and environmental benefits of drinking that coffee in a reusable ceramic cup or drinking glass rather than a disposable paper or plastic cup. Even taking into account the impacts of manufacturing and hundreds of washings, using glass and ceramic cups reduces the amount of energy, water use, air emissions, water pollution, and solid waste by between 85 and 99 percent. They also contribute considerable economic savings for cafe owners as well.[135]

While a simple act such as avoiding a disposable coffee cup can be valuable, citizens interested in promoting vital local economies also exercise leverage and control through the foods they choose to buy. The 1990s experienced a revolution in the strengthening of "local food systems," propelled by numerous well-organized movements to create direct markets for the world's increasingly vulnerable family farmers. Farmers' markets, community-supported agriculture (CSA) arrangements, the

Slow Food network, co-ops and buyers' clubs, chefs' initiatives, and buy-local campaigns have laid the foundation for a profoundly shifting food culture. This rapidly expanding worldwide ethic is based largely upon the support of local suppliers of in-season, organic foods as an alternative to the global industrial fare one finds at typical supermarkets and fast-food restaurants.

The Farm-in-a-Box

One excellent example of such emerging arrangements is the CSA box. Community-supported agriculture is a movement that has been established in dozens of countries in the latter part of the 20th century to unite consumers with nearby farmers around the concept of locally grown, seasonal produce. In these mutually beneficial consumer/producer arrangements—also known in England as "box schemes" and in Japan as "food with a farmer's face"—members pay an agreed-upon advance fee to farmers before the growing season begins (a form of interest-free loans). In return, each week throughout the growing season, members receive a share of fruits and vegetables and sometimes other items. The food is typically grown without pesticides and provides enough for two adults and two children. Boxes are delivered to a centralized drop-off or pick-up location, or even to the doorstep, overflowing with fruits, vegetables, leafy greens, and sometimes other essentials, like eggs, flowers, or honey. Packaging is minimal, usu-

ally a cardboard bushel box that can be reused again and again. This is nothing less than a total systems approach to food distribution, consumption, and packaging.

Food Miles

In addition to ecolabels such as organic, biodynamic, grass-fed, shade grown, and fair trade, "food miles" is another mechanism being used to qualify a food item's product history. A given item's food-mile factor measures the distance it has traveled between the field and dinner table. Prior to the ratification of the North American Free Trade Agreement, the average distance a typical produce item traveled in the United States was estimated at 1,300 miles.[136] This is widely acknowledged today to be far too conservative, with some estimates averaging upward of 2,000 miles.

Calculating the food miles of packaged and processed foods can be far more complex. Consider this abbreviated account of a jar of yogurt, made in Germany with Polish strawberries. "Yogurt cultures came from northern Germany, corn and wheat flour from the Netherlands, sugar beets from east Germany, and the labels and aluminum covers for the jars were being made over 300 kilometers away. Only the jar and the milk were made locally. . . . But there are a whole range of further hidden miles that these calculations ignore. The aluminum for the yogurt jar lids has come from mines many thousands of miles from the packaging plant. The machinery used for packaging the yogurt had to be brought from Switzerland or Britain.... So the circle widens, at every point adding to the real costs of the yogurt, but which do not get added to the price and instead must be paid for in other ways at other times."[137]

Buy-Local Campaigns

In the United States, an organized national coalition known as Food Routes has spawned buy-local campaigns in numerous regions of the country to address the issues that surround faraway food production. In the summer of 2003, for example, the Maine Organic Farming and Gardening Association launched a campaign encouraging 10 percent of state residents to purchase $10 worth of produce from Maine farmers each week throughout the growing season. This, they reasoned, could pump $100 million into the regional farm economy. On the other side of the continent, the California Alliance with Family Farmers is targeting school cafeterias, college campuses, and other institutional procurement agencies in order to forge long-term markets for regional medium- to large-scale growers. Considering that the U.S. Department of Agriculture spends some $16 billion on school lunch subsidies, such an ambitious initiative could direct millions of dollars in appropriations into regional production loops. In addition to supporting farmers growing healthy foods, these are just the sort of medium-distance, repeat business rela-

tionships that can also make returnable transport packaging (RTP) systems financially viable. RTPs are durable, often-collapsible and stackable trays and containers that can be used again and again.

Materials Exchange Programs

Similar regional coordination is taking place in other endeavors, including residential building, materials exchanges, and even decentralized energy production. Slowly, architects, contractors, and homeowners have been pioneering a new wave of green architecture, moving toward building solutions that are defined by local climate, nearby materials, and vernacular designs. Other organizations are focused on facilitating the reuse of perfectly good materials and byproducts through the development of (open and regional) "waste exchanges." The organizational structures of these waste exchanges are diverse—ranging from government-funded agencies to nonprofits, to for-profit businesses, as well as alliances of all of the above. Their goals, however, are similar: to divert materials from dumpsters and landfills by brokering wastes and byproducts such as plastics, rubber, pallets, crates, textiles, wood, paper, metals, glass, and other items. From an economic perspective, these programs work by creating opportunities for reuse of materials as well as by reducing disposal costs for participants.

The New York Waste-Match (NYWM) is typical of a burgeoning number of materials management and exchange services. According to a profile in *In Business* magazine, the NYWM has partnered with various agencies, departments, and businesses to build a dynamic materials exchange database. It has worked to educate regional businesses about the combined benefits of waste reduction and resource recovery programs. Most participants receive tangible savings—between $3,000 and $15,000 per year.[138] Sometimes these recovery exchanges mean the difference between a company staying in an area or leaving simply because of the increasing costs of garbage disposal fees.

As one might expect, many of the diverted commodities are packaging materials. A Long Island computer equipment maker, for example, shipped used plastic bags to a Queens sheet metal fabricator to incorporate in packaging. A Brooklyn manufacturer sold packing crates to a Queens shipping company to be refashioned into custom shipping cases.[139] In the case of Three Guys from Brooklyn, a large wholesale and retail produce distributor, previously comingled and landfilled boxes were separated into baled corrugated (recyclable) and wax-coated cardboard (landfilled). Dewatering equipment drastically reduced the volumes of spoiled produce, further slashing landfill bills. Altogether, this thorough materials audit and action strategy saved $158,980 in yearly disposal costs.[140] Similarly, Krinos Foods, an importer of Greek delicacies such as olives, feta cheese, peppers, and oil, was able to save over $30,000 in

annual disposal fees by selling pallets to reconditioners and offering free pick-up of HDPE drums, stretch film, metals, paper packaging, and other recyclable materials.[141]

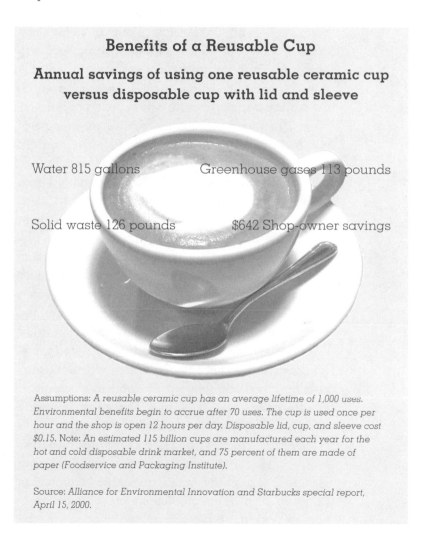

Benefits of a Reusable Cup

Annual savings of using one reusable ceramic cup versus disposable cup with lid and sleeve

Water 815 gallons   Greenhouse gases 113 pounds

Solid waste 126 pounds $642 Shop-owner savings

Assumptions: A reusable ceramic cup has an average lifetime of 1,000 uses. Environmental benefits begin to accrue after 70 uses. The cup is used once per hour and the shop is open 12 hours per day. Disposable lid, cup, and sleeve cost $0.15. Note: An estimated 115 billion cups are manufactured each year for the hot and cold disposable drink market, and 75 percent of them are made of paper (Foodservice and Packaging Institute).

Source: Alliance for Environmental Innovation and Starbucks special report, April 15, 2000.

Harnessing Youth Energy:
The Barn Owl Box Project

Students are also getting into the act. Since the mid-1990s, Merced High School, 100 miles south of Sacramento in California's Central Valley, has been the locus of an unusual packaging recovery program. Each day of the school year, for one 51-minute period, the students of Merced High's wood-shop class transform castaway wooden packaging crates into products highly valued in their rural community. The crates, discarded by fruit and nut growers and otherwise rerouted from landfills, are cut, planed, sanded, and later assembled into houses specifically designed to attract barn owls. They are then sold throughout farming regions in California and surrounding western states.

The program, called the Raptor Works, was started by now-retired shop teacher and volunteer biologist Steve Simmons, and it has generated complex benefits with ripple effects throughout the local community. It starts by making a value-added product out of what was formerly considered packaging waste. In this case, salvaged wooden transport bins provide ¾-inch plywood raw materials for the boxes free of charge. Simmons' specially designed habitats enjoy nearly a 95 percent occupancy rate, which is good news for grape and row-crop farmers. The barn owls consume significant numbers of gophers, voles, and other rodents that damage crops. This creates a natural, local solution to a pest problem that might otherwise be

dealt with by applying poisons that can travel up the food chain. In addition to salvaging perfectly reusable wooden crates, the students also line the boxes with wood shavings as nesting materials. The yearly total adds up to 8 cubic yards, which requires collecting all the shavings from the high school's four wood-shop classes as well as from those of schools outside the district.

By all accounts, the barn owl box project has been an economic home run. Simmons set up the Raptor Works as an entrepreneurial class where students establish the rules of participation and learn all the skills of running a business, from manufacturing to marketing, distribution, and quality control. He had no idea when he started, however, of the niche that he tapped into. "I never dreamed there would be such a demand for boxes in agricultural communities," says Simmons.[142] Over an eight-year period, the classes have made and sold more than 8,000 boxes, earning over $150,000 that was returned to students in the form of scholarships for post-secondary education and other career pursuits. Their product line has been expanded to include nesting boxes for wood ducks, kestrels, screech owls, and bluebirds.

A conservationist who has been concerned about the fate of wildlife throughout his life, Simmons' barn owl box project is an outstanding example of the power of setting a simple idea to practice. Yet it also has profound ripple effects throughout the community by engaging the younger generation, reusing overlooked resources, and valuing nature.

Citizen Power

Certainly the less packaging we consume, the lower the impact on habitat, resources, energy production, and particulate pollution. While we may not be able to limit the amount of packaging that accompanies an occasional major purchase—such as a television, computer, or refrigerator—there are things that we can proactively do on a daily basis to minimize the damage. Depending on our situations, we can live first and foremost like citizens of a village or town or city, looking to our respective regions for sources of perishable fruits, vegetables, meats, dairy, and other products. We can carry refillable mugs and water bottles, take the time to eat in rather than take out, consolidate shopping errands intelligently, always have a stash of cloth shopping bags handy, donate shock-absorbing packaging materials to businesses that will reuse them, and write letters to our favorite companies or least-favorite "bad wrappers." Backyard compost systems can supplement or take the place of municipal organic collection. Buying in bulk can reduce transport and packaging impacts. According to the University of Michigan School of Packaging, the typical American family can reduce its waste by 285 pounds per year simply by purchasing staple items such as cereal, soft drinks, and tuna in bulk. Doing so delivers economic savings as well.[143]

Yet it also bears asking: can we really expect to buy our way out of present predicaments with green or smart consumption? Certainly consumer power is one of the most profound forces in the world today. Profound because consumer spending reportedly accounts for roughly two-thirds of all economic activity in the United States.[144] Profound because the potential for alliances among parents, institutional and government procurement agencies, LOHAS (upward of 70 million Americans classified by "lifestyles of health and sustainability"), students, boycotting activists, and millions of others is palpable and effective. Yet illusive because in a world of consolidations and diminishing retail outlets, of widening gaps between haves and have-nots, it is difficult to assess how much choice the easily manipulated public truly has.

It may seem inevitable to some that most household items will one day be bought at Wal-Mart, that most countries will succumb to being fast-food nations, and that Starbucks will appear in every city in the world, but there is another economic force mobilizing around the world: the consuming and organizing power of local economies. "With proper planning, local production systems can be more material- and energy-efficient than global production systems," says writer and researcher Warren Karlenzig. "When people buy fresh food from their local farmers, build with local materials, or design based on local resource availability and climate, they keep money from leaking out of the community or region."[145] This can help build true long-term economic security as well as a vibrant sense of place.

Farms of the future? Windmills now symbolize a source of clean, abundant, renewable energy.

A FUTURE

Is packaging a problem? Yes, absolutely. Is it humanity's biggest challenge? Not even close. Unfortunately, we have far larger problems, although packaging contributes to them as well. Can we do better? Let's hope so. As this journey outside the box has demonstrated, there are already global and local forces at work to reshape the way we produce, package, consume, dispose, and sometimes reuse the stuff of everyday things. But as long as the costs of raw materials continue to be staggeringly low, burying waste in holes in the ground will have strong economic justifications.

Other beguiling questions and immense challenges lie before us. Can we develop economies that honor humanity and protect all species for future generations? Are cradle-to-cradle manufacturing systems—ordered into classes of degradable biological materials and benign industrial materials—an achievable solution to economic systems that fail to account for external costs, such as environmental degradation? What roles will landfills and incinerators play in a world brimming with large urban human populations? How will we find ways to make agriculture and forestry practices less damaging

Critics argue that windmill installations are not free of visual or wildlife impacts.

BEYOND THE BOX

and to develop highly efficient, renewable energy systems that abide by the tenets of natural capital? To what extent can standardization contribute to a more resourceful world in terms of legislation, resource recovery, decentralized processing infrastructures, and commonly accepted ecological principles? Can the study of natural systems and biomimicry teach us to design and make things in a more Earth-intelligent manner?

There is no doubt that paper and plastic will have a place in our world for decades to come. What remains unknown is whether we can make conscious choices that promote healthy air, clean and abundant water, noble employment, sustainable local economies, and vibrant cultures. There is no reason that disparate efforts can't take place simultaneously to speed reform. What remains essential is that our attempted solutions address both the product and the package in an integrated, systemic manner. Profound reforms will require bold goals and an acceptance of short-term investments in research and education. With a balance between action and observation, and a commitment to "try, monitor, adjust, and try again," change can be a dynamic and energizing force.

Bad Wraps

We've all had the experience of tearing into a much-anticipated package, only to have to dig through an absurd amount of packing material to find the object inside. Many of us also settle for that occasional, all-too-convenient packaged food item, only to be left with an indestructible container that's destined to spend an eternity in a landfill. Inefficient use of materials, excessive empty space, and over-engineering are just a few telltale signs of blatantly bad wraps. Here are a few examples.

Packaging That Works

Looking back on the examples presented in this book, it is possible to create a list of factors that might help us evaluate packaging. An environmentally preferable package . . .

- Is designed from a whole-systems perspective, including its material sourcing, use, manufacture, distribution, and ultimate disposal

- Is information-intensive as opposed to material- and energy-intensive

- Contains no ancient forest fibers; if virgin-wood fibers are used, preferably they come from a known source or have been certified by an independent, third-party sustainable forestry organization

- Avoids hazardous chlorine compounds, heavy metals, and other persistent toxins

- Can be reprocessed within local and regional resource loops whenever possible

- Uses as few material types as possible and breaks down into reusable or separable materials (designed for disassembly)

- Contains as much post-consumer recycled or agricultural waste materials as possible when appropriate

- Has been optimized through some form of life-cycle analysis to minimize resource extraction, energy and water consumption, and manufacturing and transportation impacts

- Considers how a redesigned or reformulated product can affect the amount of packaging needed

- Is only as large as it needs to be

- Is as light as possible without compromising product safety

- Is responsibly produced throughout its entire packaging chain

- Is safe for all species and habitats

- Can be refilled, reconstituted, eaten (even by bugs), upcycled as a value-added product (such as a building material) or have some other meaningful extended life

- Is derived from renewable biological and natural systems as much as possible

- Complies with the highest current international standards for packaging and extended producer responsibility

- Attempts to close the gap between the life span of its materials and the shelf-life of the product it packages

- Is packaged according to its particular delivery system both to and from use

- Identifies all materials and components

What You Can Do

1 Carry a mug. Even taking into account the impacts of manufacturing and hundreds of washings, glass and ceramic cups reduce the amount of energy, water use, air emissions, water pollution, and solid waste by between 85 and 99 percent.

2 Carry your own water bottle and install a home filtering system. Since the early 1970s, there has been an explosion in the bottled water industry. Up to 25 percent of bottled water is now sold to export markets. Solid-waste problems are mounting because of a lack of opportunities to reuse bottles. In some cases, acquifers in farming regions have been depleted in order to produce bottled water for export.

3 Keep a stash of cloth shopping bags handy. The proper answer to the paper versus plastic dilemma is still "neither." Cultivate a stash of bags that can be reused hundreds of times and last for decades rather than becoming disposal burdens or litter.

4 Minimize take-out packaging. Try staying at a restaurant rather than eating packaged food on the go. It's safer and can minimize disposable packaging. The problem is so extreme that some Asian countries have banned certain types of disposable food packaging.

5 Intelligently plan shopping trips. Consolidate shopping trips effectively so that you make the most of your time and fossil-fuel expenditures. Consider whether you really need an item before you buy it.

6 Become a backyard composter. You can turn vegetarian food scraps, yard trimmings, and even certain forms of packaging, such as soiled pizza cartons and other ink-free paper materials, into soil amendments for your garden.

7 Support local farmers. Purchasing fresh foods from local farmers is a great way to support the local economy and provide healthier food for your family. Community-supported agriculture arrangements supply weekly deliveries of fresh, organic foods in reusable cartons.

8 Don't wrap gifts for pets. Landfill-bound trash and packaging waste spikes between 25 and 30 percent in the United States in the period between Thanksgiving and the first week of the New Year. The extra waste mounds up to about 25 million tons of garbage. Give gifts that support your ethical values and consider wrapping them minimally, in reused materials, or even in reusable shopping bags or containers.

9 Support producers who effectively package goods. Vote with your pocketbook and a mind toward minimizing waste and supporting a world of health and beauty. Companies that minimally package goods or use containers with high post-consumer recycled content deserve high marks. Learn your materials: number 1 and 2 plastics are the most recycled. Numbers 3 through 7 are seldom recycled, and many, if not most, end up in landfills.

10 Establish a reusable packaging policy for your household. Complete a household packaging audit. Create household systems that emphasize reusable alternatives, from lunch boxes and leftovers to storage containers. Styrofoam peanuts, shredded paper, and sealed air bags can be reused or donated to local companies.

11 Bulk up. Households can significantly reduce their packaging and save money with bulk purchases of staple items such as cereal, soft drinks, tuna, and cleaning solutions.

12 Know your dump. The best knowledge about the waste stream is local. It starts with a visit to the local landfill, recycling center, salvage yards, and other sites and learning which materials are reused, which are discarded, and which you can reuse yourself.

13 Be clear about your ecological footprint. No amount of "smart resource management" can get us around the impacts of sustained human population growth and rising consumption levels. Let packaging serve as one of many factors to gauge and inform whether or not consumption patterns are compatible with your values and hopes for the planet.

Wraps at a Glance

The following section is intended to describe briefly the functional attributes as well as some of the potential environmental challenges of individual packaging materials and systems. In order to obtain more accurate information on any given packaging choice, a complete assessment should be made. That would include a life-cycle analysis of some sort; a study of where and how materials have been sourced and the conditions of processing and manufacture; and the potential for recovery and reprocessing in the places where products will be sold. A number of helpful resources for life-cycle analyses can be found in Appendix C. In the meantime, this section can serve as both a rough (unscientific) guide to some specific packaging types as well as a glimpse of the many kinds of packages used on a daily basis.

Polystyrene Foam
Advantages: Excellent strength-to-weight cushioning capacity. New blowing agents no longer contain ozone-depleting CFCs. Lower energy and manufacturing impacts than paper in some cases. Sony, in Japan, is developing a remolding process based upon a citrus-based (limonene) solvent.
Challenges: Petroleum product. Toxic chemicals could be released through low-tech incineration. Bulky and difficult to reuse. Usually goes to landfill but could potentially be recycled in certain building materials. Reuse should favor grinding over remelting. Unfavorable image.

FRESH PRODUCE PACKS

Wooden Crate
Advantages: Made primarily from low-grade materials for one-time long-distance shipping. Potential for reuse, depending on durability of crate, workmanship, and user. Could potentially be made from certified forest products.
Challenges: Forest practices could degrade ecosystems. Because of lack of durability, the opportunities for reuse are low. Could potentially be chipped for energy generation or landscaping cover. Normally sent to landfill or incinerator at end of life.

Molded Pulp

Advantages: Can be formed to fit. Normally made of high-content recycled, unbleached newsprint. Potentially compostable. Potential to contain high percentages of agricultural residues. Static-free. Can be certified processed chlorine-free. Good for high-end applications.

Challenges: Not as durable as corrugated. Heavier in weight than foam.

Deformable Shape Packaging

Advantages: Could possibly be made from 100 percent post-consumer recycled materials. Geometric spring system works well under heavy loads.

Challenges: A bit more expensive than some other shock-absorbing packaging materials.

Die-Cut Corrugated

Advantages: Potentially high post-consumer recycled material, though most fibers will originate in forests. Highly recyclable throughout the world, though limited applications for reuse. Could be certified as totally chlorine-free or processed chlorine-free. FSC certification also possible for virgin content.

Challenges: Somewhat material-intensive and heavier than plastic or foam. More expensive than foam due to higher labor costs.

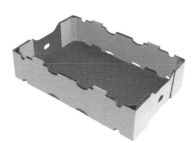

Wax-Coated Produce Container

Advantages: Could contain a certain amount of post-consumer fibers. Can be downcycled into fireplace logs.

Challenges: Forest product. Wax coating makes it difficult to reprocess. Normally sent to landfill or incinerator.

Returnable Produce Container

Advantages: Can be used many times. Also serves as an in-store display tray. Made of a durable material that can be reprocessed into something else at the end of life.

Challenges: In order to achieve payback, RPCs must be reused by the original customer a minimum number of times. The key prohibitive factor in the United States is the decentralized, long-distance food system, which often means high costs for returning empties back to centers of production before being put on the road again. Must be carefully washed before reuse.

CSA Box

Advantages: Community-supported agriculture farms use these containers for weekly shipments to member customers. They contain minimally packaged fresh produce and can be used many times before being recycled.

BEVERAGE CONTAINERS

Foil Pouch
Advantages: Convenient, lightweight, and easily compressible.
Challenges: These multilayered, nonrecyclable materials are destined for the landfill. Soft-drink companies are rapidly adopting this packaging system, often to package a high-fructose product.

Single-Serving Plastic Bottle
Advantages: Flexible and lightweight. Sometimes burned for energy generation.
Challenges: Only #1 and #2 have high-end recycling markets. Plastic #3–#7 lack a strong recycling infrastructure. Pollute waterways and marine areas. Oxygen barriers, fillers, and other coatings on bottles prohibit recycling. Plasticizers and other additives can potentially be toxic.

Gable-Top Carton
Advantages: Long-distance solution. Can be repulped and downcycled into paper towels and tissue paper at end of life.
Challenges: Only reprocessed in certain markets. Can rot if not collected and reprocessed in a timely manner.

LOOSE-FILL PACKAGING

Air Pockets
Advantages: Easily storable and usable. Could be made with recovered post-consumer plastics.
Challenges: Currently no outlet for recycling.

Air Systems
Advantages: It is reported that replacing Styrofoam peanuts or shredded paper with inflatable systems can reduce waste by up to 90 percent. Savings on material and shipping costs possible. Compresses easily in landfill.
Challenges: Requires storage space for reuse.

Bubble Wrap
Advantages: Easy to store for reuse. Forms to fit. Popping bubbles entertains children but afterward leaves the material worthless.
Challenges: Can't be recycled currently, but could be made of a post-consumer recycled or degradable plastic.

Popcorn Fiber Wrap
Advantages: Made from popcorn. Could potentially be grown and certified organic. Biodegradable.
Challenges: Farming practices should be considered. Could be attractive to rodents and other animals. Not water resistant.

Aluminum
Advantages: Easy to recycle and has fairly brisk recycling markets in many areas of the world. Very strong material.
Challenges: Virgin aluminum is extremely energy-intensive. The mining and production of virgin aluminum has heavy impacts on habitats, particularly aquatic systems. Ultimately, it rusts and breaks down. While recycling does save considerable energy, the cans are not refillable.

Single-Serving Glass Bottle
Advantages: Highly recyclable. Strong markets for glass recycling in many regions of the country. Efficient use of materials.
Challenges: Heavier than many plastics and often not seen as desirable for long-distance transport of beverages. Doesn't biodegrade.

Refillable Glass Bottle
Advantages: Highly reusable. Ultimately recyclable. Works on a refill deposit system.
Challenges: Heavy weight limits the glass bottle to short-distance transport and therefore favors local food producers. Requires producer and consumer commitment or strict legislation.

Polystyrene Peanuts
Advantages: High strength-to-weight ratio. Less energy and manufacturing impacts than paper. Inexpensive. Water resistant. Good material for cushioning and thermal applications.
Challenges: A petroleum byproduct. High levels of static electricity. Not easy to store, and therefore very frustrating for user. High litter factor. Last for decades.

Cornstarch Peanuts
Advantages: Short shelf-life as they dissolve in water and naturally decompose. Made of a surplus agricultural crop.
Challenges: Moisture sensitive. Rodents like them. The environmental impacts of corn production are significant.

Shredded Paper
Advantages: Made from post-consumer waste, a large component of landfills. Sometimes used as a filler within padded envelopes.
Challenges: Unfortunately, it is not conveniently stored and therefore may be difficult to collect for reprocessing.

Perforated Paper
Advantages: Can be made without chlorine bleach. Can be made from 100 percent post-consumer waste. Reusable and recyclable in many areas of the world.
Challenges: Forest-based product and should not come from ancient or intact habitats.

TRANSPORT PALLETS

Wood Pallets
Advantages: Large manufacturing infrastructure exists to produce pallets. Recovery and reuse is slowly expanding.
Challenges: Not always made for durability. Often break and split with wear. After just one or two uses these are normally chipped and used as alternative daily cover in landfill. Internationally, pallets must be heat- or chemically treated to ward off Asian long-horned beetle and other exotic pests. Untreated pallets are significant components of landfills.

Returnable Transit Systems
Advantages: Used in pallet pools to prevent pallets from otherwise going into waste streams. Money savings possible. Creates jobs in reuse.
Challenges: Wood is a forest product and should be certified as sustainably harvested.

FSC-Certified Wood Pallets
Advantages: Environmentalists agree this third-party certification system promotes best management practices. Pallets are a high-value use of small-diameter trees thinned from woodlots.
Challenges: Still coming from working forests. Higher cost of raw materials.

BAGS

Degradable Shopping Bag
Advantages: Made of a renewable resource (corn-based plastic) that biodegrades in a matter of weeks. Provides an alternative to petroleum-based plastic. Can be used to dispose of food scraps in municipal composting programs.
Challenges: A product of industrial agriculture. Inks could potentially contain heavy metals that would migrate as the bag decomposes.

Canvas Tote
Advantages: Long life. Could be made from post-industrial factory scraps and potentially from organically grown cotton. Easily washed and tucked away for shopping trips. Very strong.
Challenges: Industrially farmed cotton is one of the largest consumers of pesticides and fertilizers. Requires consumers to remember to always have them handy.

Paper or Plastic

Cardboard Pallets
Advantages: Half the weight of wooden pallets. Can be made very strong. Can be reprocessed into other paper materials after use. Could contain a certain amount of post-consumer fibers.
Challenges: Forest product. Possible problems with humidity and moisture.

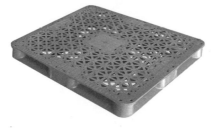

Plastic Pallets
Advantages: Take the place of disposable wooden pallets, a significant contributor to the waste stream. Provide a systems solution to the packaging crisis. Do not harbor pests.
Challenges: Petroleum product. Costs are higher than disposable wood containers and therefore limit investment and require a certain number of repeat shipments to justify costs.

Paper
Advantages: Can often contain a high percentage of processed chlorine-free post-consumer fibers. Can be reused and eventually recycled.
Challenges: Materials still originate in forests. Heavier in weight and not as strong as other disposable options.

Plastic Disposable
Advantages: Lightweight, strong, reusable to a point. Relatively energy efficient processing. Water resistant.
Challenges: Petroleum product. Extremely high litter factor and relatively poor public image. Some countries have banned altogether or levied point-of-sale fees for the usage of disposable plastic bags.

> In an environment that is screwed up visually, physically, and chemically, the best and simplest thing that architects, industrial designers, planners, etc. could do for humanity would be to stop working entirely. But it seems to me that we can go beyond not working at all and work positively.
>
> —Victor Papanek, author, professor, and early advocate for environmental and social responsibility within the design professions

A Future Beyond the Box

Beyond-the-Box Packaging Solutions

What makes a better package? Is it the effective design, durability, or degradability, the appropriate use of materials (or lack thereof?), the fact that it's been made with recovery, reprocessing, or reuse in mind, or all of the above? One thing is certain. A good wrap begins with a sound product that contributes to a healthful world. From start to finish, it aims at optimizing the materials, processing, and energy needed to produce it. At best, a package can be upcycled with a minimum of effort and energy, such as a jelly jar to a drinking glass, or composted or recycled safely and efficiently.

In an age when packaging and processing are increasingly being used to "add value" to basic commodities, we've tried to uncover a number of packaging solutions that combine form, function, and fundamental commitment to lower environmental impacts. Included are a few noteworthy consumer products made from recovered packaging materials as well as innovative concepts and systems that may contribute to positive change. This section greatly benefited from the sleuthing of leading-edge wraps and photos by international eco-design expert Anne Chick.

Design for Recycling. The Italian beverage producer Sarda Acqua Minerali's lightweight Ecobottle features an innovative "design for recycling" concept. The bottle and cap are made from 100 percent PET plastic. With no labels, inks, or glues, the manufacturer claims a raw material and energy savings of up to 15 percent. A seal sleeve that wraps the screw cap provides printable space for the bar code and colors that identify the product. Like many mineral waters, the Ecobottle is marketed in shrink-wrapped packs of six with a handle for easy transport. The shrink-wrap film can be printed with branding and product information. When customers buy the Ecobottle, they receive a free, purposely made tool that cuts the bottle in two with a simple circular movement. Nothing needs to be thrown away as the screw cap can stay on the bottle. The Ecobottle's double conical shape, tapered at both top and bottom, allows the lower cut-off part of the bottle to be tucked up inside the upper part. The low neck profile affords a tight concentration of stacked bottles—full or empty.
www.ecobottle.com

Returnable Transit Package. The Riverside Strong Box breaks down to one-quarter of its original size for return shipping. A disposable inner liner holds 3,000 gallons of liquid materials, replacing palletized shipments in much smaller individual drums or containers. It also stacks eight high and can be used as many as 700 times.
www.riverside.bc.ca

Dissolvable Foam. Over 10 years and $300 million in progress, EarthShell's mission is to green up one of the waste stream's daily villains—the fast- food clamshell. EarthShell blends starch from potato discards or wheat gluten with limestone and special fillers, then cooks them into degradable one-way containers for the food service industry. In taking on single-use polystyrene foam, one of EarthShell's biggest challenges has been the need to develop new generations of manufacturing equipment. According to the Environmental Protection Agency, 800,000 tons of clamshells cups and other plastic packaging were thrown out in the United States in 2001. Company officials say the package could be eaten in desperation, but they don't recommend it.
www.earthshell.com

Edible Wraps? Eager to find new uses for agricultural surpluses, researchers at the USDA Western Regional Resource Center in Albany, California, have come up with a new packaging category functional food wraps. Films are made from pureed fruits and vegetables—apples, peaches, broccoli, carrots—using an aqueous casting process. The next step is to extrude these purees into more rigid forms. Edible fruit and vegetable films are expected to be introduced in 2005 with potential applications for meat wraps, breath fresheners, and packaging. Suggests the USDA's Tara McHugh: "Imagine apple-film-wrapped pork chops that go from the refrigerator to the stove where the film melts into an apple glaze on the meat."
www.pw.usda.gov

A Future Beyond the Box

Concentrate Pouch. European extended producer responsibility packaging legislation has led to a wave of packaging and product design reform. In the case of this laundry detergent, the product has been concentrated and its package minimized. The pouch is designed for easy pouring into an existing container. These packaging solutions reduce materials, transport impacts, shelf space, and money.

Label-Less, Refillable Beer Bottle. The European brewing industry has been marked by decreasing sales and increasing legislative pressures to adopt or sustain refillable packaging systems, particularly in northern Europe. Brauerei C & A Veltins, a German brewery, has responded to these issues with an innovative refillable glass bottle. Conceived by its in-house design team for the company's Gastronomy beer brand, the bottle sports no label but relies solely on the beverage container to communicate the brand. This is achieved through the distinctive shape of the beer bottle and its tactile features. The bottle has also been designed for optimum efficiency in the refill, storage, and transportation processes. The label-less container eliminates the process of removing old labels within the packaging refilling system. A broad opening increases the efficiency of the filling operation. And a squat, rather than a tall, neck reduces volume, thereby optimizing efficiency in storage and transportation. The German packaging industry recognized this innovative design by awarding the brewing company one of its prestigious 2002 design prizes.
www.veltins.de

Mimicking Nature's Design. What wisdom can designers glean from the patterns of nature? Researchers at the Montana-based Biomimicry Guild believe that observing the ways that plants and animals package various items can reveal valuable new concepts for our own product protection and delivery systems. A pelican's pouch can expand to scoop 3 gallons of water in a single swipe before neatly collapsing. Other concepts that nature might inspire: packages that self-repair, on-demand packaging, or packages that use the space-optimizing designs of spirals and leaf structures to minimize necessary materials and energy.
www.biomimicry.org

Optimized Hot Beverage Container.
Each day an estimated 100 million cups are consumed to fulfill America's coffee habits. Because coffee tastes far better at temperatures around 200 degrees Fahrenheit, manufacturers have moved toward polystyrene foam, double paper cups, or single cups with a ribbed sleeve that is roughly one-third of the surface area of a regular cup. The GeoCup, brainchild of architect Tim Johnson, has two vertical "cool zones" for finger placement that add only 7 percent more material to the design. Other features of the GeoCup, which is slated for release in 2005, include the use of plantation wood fibers or agricultural tree-free content, and "benign chemistry" to minimize toxics in paper and lid production.
www.geocup.com

Reverse Vending Machine. TOMRA is a beverage vending machine in reverse. You place in it an empty bottle or can and receive a voucher for the refund. An increase in refillable bottle laws could mean that machines like these will have a role in worldwide collection systems.
www.tomra.com

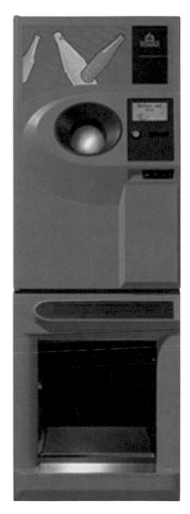

Nonchlorine-Bleached Pint. Introduced in early 1999, Ben & Jerry's Eco-Pint container was just the first phase in a long-term overhaul of the conventional ice cream container. Work on the Eco-Pint initially stemmed from a single goal—eliminating chlorine from the company's packaging. Standard production relies on chlorine compounds as bleaching agents during papermaking, a process responsible for discharging large volumes of organochlorine-laced waste water. Among these are carcinogenic and highly toxic dioxins. Currently the Eco-Pint is made from 100 percent, nonchlorine bleached, virgin-wood paperboard sourced from Riverside out of Louisiana. (The Eco-Pint is still made of virgin wood as required by law and still goes to the landfill because of its petroleum-based vapor and moisture barriers.) Ben & Jerry's researchers and packaging designers are searching for alternatives to the federally mandated food-grade polyethylene coating. Addressing inks and glues, which can also contain chlorine compounds, should follow. The ultimate goal would be a 100 percent compostable cup, says Andrea Asch, manager of natural resource use for Ben & Jerry's. Until then, there's always a sugar cone.
www.benjerry.com

Packaging Health and Beauty. For nearly a decade, Aveda has been dematerializing its packaging—by lightweighting containers as well as by maximizing the post-consumer recycled (PCR) content of plastics such as HDPE, polypropylene, glass, and boxboard. With product and packaging designers interacting closely, Aveda has succeeded in raising the PCR content in much of its packaging to between 80 and 100 percent, with very little containing less than 50 percent. A 10-year effort to maximize the post-consumer resin content and redesign shampoo bottles to make them as thin as possible now saves the company about $1 million per year. Aveda's Uruku lipstick package, below, contains multiple optimized elements. The molded pulp case is made from 100 percent recycled newsprint with a 100 percent PCR paperboard sleeve. The accessory case is a blend of 30 percent flax shives (a crop residue) and 70 percent polypropylene (containing 90 percent PCR content). The lipstick canister itself is replaceable. (This system works: lipstick refills reportedly out-sell complete cases by three to one!) The lipstick cartridge is sheathed in an aluminum sleeve (with up to 65 percent PCR aluminum) and contains two other plastic elements made of recycled high-impact polystyrene with 88 percent PCR content.
www.aveda.com

Fresh Pack Minus the Wax. To many, the wax-lined corrugated box is symbolic of produce, meat, poultry, or fish, packed in ice for maximum freshness. The wax coating allows for foods to be "hydro-cooled" without soggy cardboard. But a wax-coated corrugated box's virtue is also its bane. Because it is extremely expensive to separate the vapor barrier from the box fibers, these containers are almost assuredly bound for the landfill or incinerator. For supermarkets and food distributors, this can translate into tens of thousands of dollars in yearly disposal fees. If and when the recycling stars align, wax-coated corrugated can be pressed into decorative fireplace logs that burn with a single match. According to Richard Farinelli of the Newark Group, one of the oldest recycled-box producers in the United States, wax coatings pose other concerns.[146] Volatile organic compounds released in the manufacture of these synthetic materials are serious air contaminants.

Using a European technology with a 15-year track record, the Newark Group produces wax-free, waterproof solid board containers. The boxes themselves are made from old corrugated containers and recycled newsprint pressed into solid fiber panels. A "special coating" enables the boxes to withstand the rigors of ice packing as well as high moisture levels. That same coating dissolves upon repulping, making the fresh packs completely recyclable. According to Farinelli, premiums for the wax-free boxes range from 0 to 5 percent, with smaller sizes being more price competitive than larger ones. Compared with the disposal fees, the potential cost savings are significant.

Initial markets? "Organic farmers are very interested in packing their high-value products in something besides a wax-coated box," says Farinelli.
www.newarkgroup.com

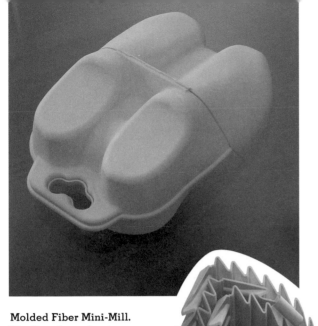

Molded Fiber Mini-Mill.
The Regale packaging concept brings 100-year-old egg-carton technology into the computer age. Through the aid of rapid prototype technology and injection molding, the company can now produce molds and packaging previously limited to shallow forms such as egg cartons and apple trays. Regale's idea is to establish mini-mills that can use the local waste stream as the primary source of materials. Agricultural fibers and crop residues could also be incorporated into the blend. At right is a material-efficient shock-absorbing corner cushion. Above is a prototype for a shoe box that is custom sized and can be reused.
www.regale.com

Refill Gladness. The inspiration for Laurie Brown's refill stations derived from observing customers dutifully returning bottles to her own retail venue, Restore the Earth Store. Back in 1991, the Minnesota-based entrepreneur began manufacturing her own brand of plant-based, nontoxic household cleaning products. These general-purpose, laundry, and kitchen products featured ingredients widely used in many processed natural food and personal care items: soy, coconut, and palm kernel surfactants; soy and orange solvents; corn-based acids and xanthum gum. To encourage reuse of the packaging, Brown's retail staff refilled customers' bottles by hand, offering a $1 rebate for each returned container.

Anxious to further evolve the concept, she applied for a grant from the Minnesota Office of Environmental Assistance and was awarded $70,000 as part of a program to reduce plastics and toxics. The grant covered the development of a prototype automated refill system, as well as the production and installation of six Restore refill machines in natural food stores in the Twin Cities region.

At present, the only thing that the Restore refill station doesn't do is wash bottles. The rest is straightforward. It reads the bar code, determining the product and container size. A probe descends to the bottle bottom and begins filling. Once topped off to the proper volume, a bar-coded coupon is printed, which is immediately redeemable at the checkout. The station meets all pertinent health and safety requirements.

Brown admits that the project has entailed a few steep learning curves. Copper piping is a case in point. While durable, it tends to turn certain products with alkaline ingredients, like laundry detergent, green. All in all, however, the machines refill bottles flawlessly, and customers are well served. Some machines, she reports, have paid for themselves in as early as nine months. With patents issued, Restore is ramping up for a major production run and national distribution. Brown's sights are initially set on the 2,000-plus natural product stores throughout the country. Licensing this technology to other companies such as personal care and beverage producers is another distinct possibility.
www.restoreproducts.com

Traditional Coffee Cans. After a prolonged study of aseptic packages, lined paper bags, coated paperboard cartons, and laminated foil pouches, Mark Inman of Taylor Made Farms in Sebastapol, California, chose to pack bulk organic coffee beans in steel cans. These containers are made with significant levels of recycled materials, and there are hundreds of things you can do with them. Storage space might be an issue for businesses who choose to use pallets of steel cans, though Inman insists it is well worth the effort.
www.taylormaidfarms.com

Locally Made Produce Boxes. These reusable wooden boxes transport fresh produce from Four Season Farm in northeastern Maine to local markets within 30 miles of the farm. In defiance of cold temperatures and limited sunlight, master farmers Eliot Coleman and Barbara Damrosch grow winter crops of salad mixes, carrots, and other cool-season plants in unheated greenhouses. The boxes are durable and made from cedar cut and milled on the farm. A Maine company also made the branding iron that takes the place of a label. All winter long, Four Season Farm's high-quality produce competes with greens and other crops imported to Maine from faraway operations in California, Florida, Mexico, and other areas. And it is grown using just a fraction of the energy required to ship produce long distances.
www.fourseasonfarm.com

Reusable Tote. IKEA, the Sweden-based home furnishings corporation, receives kudos for its unassembled flat bundled product lines that keep packaging to a minimum. In many countries, customers can also buy these highly durable, highly functional shopping totes at the checkout line for a minimal cost. In the realm of shopping bags, they're in a category all their own: voluminous, multifunctional, and super sturdy.
www.ikea.com

Buy Fresh, Buy Local Campaigns.
Food Routes, a national association of sustainable agriculture organizations, launched this campaign to raise awareness for the benefits of supporting strong regional food economies. Nostalgic graphics promote the fresh, locally produced foods of family farmers from particular regions of the country. Among the many benefits of integrated local economies is the potential for reduction in packaging of all kinds.
www.foodroutes.org

Functional Tea Canister. The Tazo Tea Company produced this canister for loose-leaf teas with a lid that doubles as a tea infuser. This "mess kit for tea" is both reusable and recycleable.
www.tazo.com

PCR Fleece. Among the many products that emerged during the 1990s converting post-consumer recycled (PCR) plastic containers into higher value items, Patagonia's synthetic fleece is exceptionally noteworthy. (Plastic "lumber" is another successful category.) Introduced in 1993, the fleece is made from 90 percent recovered soda bottles (approximately 24 per pullover). In just one decade, Patagonia has recovered nearly 90 million soda bottles from the waste stream and set off a revolution in the sportswear industry. According to the company, two-thirds of the 40 billion plastic bottles consumed annually in the United States end up in landfills. In pursuit of the totally recyclable garment, the company is also using a PCR yarn for its liner materials. In addition to making conscious choices, maintaining a modest wardrobe and wearing out or passing on unwanted garments are sound strategies for responsible clothing consumption.
www.patagonia.com
www.teijin.co.jp

BUY FRESH BUY LOCAL

Upper Minnesota River Valley

WWW.PRIDEOFTHEPRAIRIE.ORG • (320) 269.2105

Cup-Handle Toothbrush. Recycline's Preserve toothbrush is composed of 100 percent recycled materials, including at least 65 percent recovered polypropylene yogurt cups. Its package can be reused as a travel case. Recycline encourages customers to return both the toothbrush and case at end of use for recycling with a postage-paid mailer. *www.recycline.com*

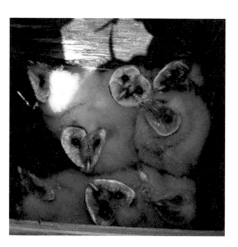

Fruit Bins to Owl Boxes. For nearly a decade, wood-shop students at Merced High School in California's Central Valley have been engaged in a unique re-packaging effort. Organized as an entrepreneurial class, the students salvage plywood from discarded fruit bins (destined for the landfill) and use them to build homes for barn owls, kestrels, wood ducks, bluebirds, and other winged creatures whose habitats have been depleted. The barn owls provide a natural biological defense against pocket gophers and other rodents that attack crops. The program, started by now-retired shop teacher Steve Simmons, has generated upward of 8,000 birdhouses purchased by West Coast farmers and over $150,000 in scholarship money for students. *www.mhs.muhsd.k12.ca.us*

Old-Fashioned Storage Tin. Italian pasta maker De Cecco offers a number of reusable tin containers that can later serve for useful attractive storage options or functional gift boxes. *www.dececco.com*

Paper or Plastic

Suggestions for Reuse. This laminated foil pouch, commonly chosen to vacuum seal and package oily and perishable coffee beans, is landfill bound. Healdsburg, California, graphic designer Chris Blum took the opportunity to suggest reuse options with Thanksgiving Coffee customers. Reusing the bag to store wet paint brushes, fishing bait, seeds and bulbs, and even broken light bulbs (for disposal) are a few of the ideas highlighted on the panel.
www.thanksgivingcoffee.com

Certified Post-Consumer Content. How can you be sure that a material really is recycled? Independent certification was obtained through Scientific Certification Systems for this durable but relatively minimal mail-order garment package.
www.scscertified.com

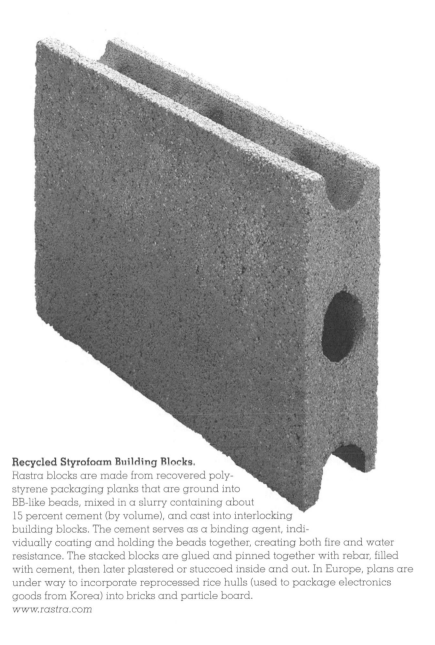

Recycled Styrofoam Building Blocks.
Rastra blocks are made from recovered polystyrene packaging planks that are ground into BB-like beads, mixed in a slurry containing about 15 percent cement (by volume), and cast into interlocking building blocks. The cement serves as a binding agent, individually coating and holding the beads together, creating both fire and water resistance. The stacked blocks are glued and pinned together with rebar, filled with cement, then later plastered or stuccoed inside and out. In Europe, plans are under way to incorporate reprocessed rice hulls (used to package electronics goods from Korea) into bricks and particle board.
www.rastra.com

APPENDIX A

Assessment of Packaging Practices

A formalized packaging optimization strategy should be a priority for any business, government agency, institution, or other entity that regularly designs, specifies, or purchases packaged items. The following checklists, recommended by eco-design expert Anne Chick, can be used by industry to evaluate and inform packaging choices. Whenever possible, locally based materials and systems should be emphasized.

Wood Reduction in Packaging

1. Does the packaging contain material from intact or endangered forests?
2. Can third-party certified virgin, post-consumer recycled, or tree-free materials be used for the wood content of packaging?

Toxics in Packaging

1. Are there toxic materials, agents, inks, adhesives, or additives in the content of the package?
2. If toxic materials or agents are present,
   (a) Can nontoxic agents or materials be substituted?
   (b) Can the toxic agents or materials be otherwise eliminated?

Packaging Elimination, Reduction, and Reuse

1. Can the package be eliminated?
2. If the package cannot be eliminated,
   (a) Can the packaging be minimized through:
      (i) Product-design changes?
      (ii) Packaging-design changes?
      (iii) Use of new or different types of lower-volume packaging?
      (iv) Lightweighting with a reduction in volume?
      (v) Elimination of secondary packaging or wrapping material?
      (vi) Decreasing the size of packaging-to-product ratio?
      (vii) Other volume reduction?
   (b) Can the package be made so that it is eliminated in using the product?
   (c) Can the package be made returnable for reuse and redistribution?
   (d) Can the package be made to be refilled by a customer or consumer from bulk or other large containers?
   (e) Can the package be made with an identifiable and valuable consumer reuse for another purpose?

Packaging Recyclability

1. Is the packaging recyclable? (Packaging is recyclable if there is a widely available, economically viable collection, processing, and marketing system for the material.)
2. If the packaging is not presently recyclable,
   (a) Can the packaging be made easier to recycle by designing it predominantly of a single material?
   (b) If the packaging is made from more than one material, can the nonhomogeneous materials be eliminated?
   (c) If nonhomogeneous materials cannot be eliminated, can they be made easily removable so as not to prevent, interfere with, or add cost to the recycling process?

Recycled Content of Packaging

1. Does the package contain the maximum feasible amount of post-consumer material (i.e., waste product or material generated by a business or consumer that has served its intended end use and is discarded for disposal or recycling)?
2. If additional post-consumer material cannot be added,
   (a) Can additional in-plant or mill scrap be added to the packaging?
   (b) Do purchasing specifications hinder the use of recycled materials?
   (c) Can purchasing specifications be modified so as to encourage the use of recycled materials in packaging?

Source Reduction

1. Can the package or any of its components be eliminated entirely (i.e., does the product really need an individual package, or can it be sold as is or in bulk)?

2. Are measurable source-reduction benefits made possible by the reuse of the package without remanufacturing?

3. (a) Can source-reduction goals be achieved by packaging geometry or structural design changes (e.g., lower packaging surface area to product volume ratios)?

   (b) Can overall packaging volume be reduced by using different packaging or container forms?

   (c) Can overall packaging weight be reduced by using different packaging or container forms?

4. (a) Does a reduction in materials in one part of the package system require as much or more materials to be used in another part of the system?

   (b) Is it possible to increase secondary or tertiary packaging to reduce primary packaging and achieve a net overall reduction?

5. Through product design changes (e.g., liquid concentrates, improved product ruggedness), can the package be redesigned to use less material without compromising the product?

6. Can the package or one of its components be designed to be safely refilled or reused by the consumer?

7. Can source-reduction goals be met by replacing a number of smaller packages with a single larger, more efficient package size (e.g., family-size or bulk containers rather than individual portion packages)?

8. Is it possible to reduce or eliminate secondary or tertiary packaging or wrapping?

9. Are customer suggestions on source-reduction possibilities for secondary and tertiary packaging throughout the distribution system solicited and encouraged?

10. Does a product or package change that results in source reduction cause an increase in solid waste in other areas (e.g., an increase in the amount of food spoiled and thrown away as a result of changing from smaller to larger packaged servings)?

11. Can source-reduction be achieved by changing the distribution process or transportation modes?

Recycling

1. (a) Does the technology exist to collect packaging from consumers and recycle it commercially?

   (b) If not, is the necessary research being conducted to develop this technology, either alone or in conjunction with industry, government, or academia?

2. (a) Is the package or its components reusable as the same item without remanufacturing?

   (b) Is there a system in place to collect and reuse these used packages?

   (c) If not, is there active development of such a system?

3. (a) Is the package recyclable (i.e., is there a system in place to recycle the package)?

   (b) If so, are instructions and a symbol used on the package to encourage recycling?

4. Can the material be identified on the package (e.g., the plastic resin recycling code) to aid collection and recycling?

5. (a) Has an in-house or in-plant resource recovery or recycling system to use waste products generated from the manufacture of the product or package been established?

   (b) If not, is there active development of such a system?

6. (a) Is the outer and inner packaging used for shipment and distribution of goods recyclable?

   (b) Has a resource recovery and recycling system been established in cooperation with customers to collect and reuse distribution packaging waste that does not reach the ultimate consumer?

   (c) If not, is there active development of such a system?

7. (a) Are programs in place to require reusable or recyclable secondary packaging from suppliers?

   (b) If not, is there active development of such programs?

8. (a) If the technology does exist to collect and recycle post-consumer packaging, are systems in place to collect and recycle the packaging?

   (b) If not, is the development of such systems being actively pursued—either alone or in conjunction with industry, government, or academia?

9. (a) Are recycling systems established for the packaging material in all the regions in which the package will be sold or distributed?

(b) If not, is participation in the creation of such regional recycling systems being pursued?

10. (a) Is there a viable commercial market for these post-consumer-recycled packaging materials?

(b) If not, are projects or programs to increase demand for this recycled material being initiated—either alone or in conjunction with industry, government, or academia?

11. (a) Is the package either mono-material or multi-material (i.e., laminated or co-extrusion)?

(b) If the package is multi-material,

(i) Are current recycling systems set up to handle them?

(ii) If there is not a recycling system in place to process the multi-material package, is the company pursuing the development of such a system—either alone or in conjunction with industry, government officials, or academia?

(iii) Is this combination of materials the most environmentally sound structural design possible without compromising product integrity?

(iv) Do the materials need to be further separated to increase their recycling value or to avoid impeding the recycling process?

12. (a) Does the primary, secondary, and/or tertiary package currently use recycled material?

(b) If so, is there a symbol and statement on the package to indicate that recycled material has been used?

13. (a) Have the effects that the use of recycled materials on the physical properties of the package (stacking strength, printing quality, etc.) been thoroughly considered?

(b) Will the use of recycled materials require more materials or an increase in the overall volume/weight of the package to maintain an acceptable level of package performance?

(c) Has the impact of recycled material use on manufacturing/production processes been researched (i.e., will recycled materials run on existing machinery, or will the use of recycled materials require significantly more energy/labor consumption)?

Disposal

1. (a) Has the package and its components (i.e., inks, dyes, pigments, stabilizers, solders, and adhesives) been made without the inclusion of toxic materials, such as heavy metals including cadmium, lead, mercury, and hexavalent chromium?

(b) If the package material currently uses toxic materials, can they be removed without compromising the package's functions?

2. (a) Can the package be landfilled safely without leaching hazardous byproducts or otherwise causing harm to the environment?

(b) If no, can the package be designed to avoid problems in landfill disposal?

3. Can the package be made smaller and/or designed to be compacted by consumers or waste management companies so that it takes up less collection/landfill space?

4. Can the package be incinerated safely to recover the energy value of the packaging materials without harmful ash residue or emissions?

5. Does the package contain sufficient combustible materials to be reprocessed for safe burning and energy recovery?

Legislative Considerations

1. Will existing or proposed legislation (i.e., package taxes, bans, deposits, solid-waste bills, etc.) affect the package?

2. (a) Does your company act in an advisory capacity to federal, state, and/or local governments to ensure that they have access to accurate packaging data?

(b) If yes, are the packaging structural design requirements fully considered by corporate lobbyists?

(c) Have you cataloged and considered all current and pending legislation in markets where your package will be sold or distributed?

Source: These preferable packaging guidelines were adapted from the Final Report of the Source Reduction Task Force of Council on New England Governors and Policy Research Center (September 1989), and from the Institute of Packaging Professionals Packaging Reduction, Recycling, and Disposal Guidelines from the Institute of Packaging Professionals (1993).

Tips on Green Packaging

The following design tips on green packaging were compiled by eco-packaging design disciple Wendy Jedlicka of the Independent Designers Network. Be sure to check Watershed Media's Web site (www.watershedmedia.org/) for updates on key green packaging resources as well as information about environmental papers, wood optimization, and other topics.

If you can't find what you want, make it yourself.
Many mills, manufacturers, and converters do custom runs—if you meet their minimum orders. For fairly large orders, consider specifying a tree-free corrugated or paperboard, or a special plastics mix featuring high post-consumer recycled content.

Tree-free papers are great for user-instructions or inserts.
Their costs can be competitive with high post-consumer recycled content or some virgin-wood pulp stocks and offer new folding/bindery opportunities due to fiber characteristics.

Make your own label stock.
This is very reasonable and can be done by most label makers in fairly small quantities. Nearly any lightweight paper makes good label stock and can be affixed with a benign adhesive. Consider using a bio-polymer or natural latex adhesive.

Designers can use their expertise to help small clients.
For example, there are several retail paperboard packaging suppliers that carry post-consumer-waste-content products, as well as scrapbooking stores that carry packaging add-ons. Small "custom" packaging runs are possible simply by choosing an appropriate off-the-shelf stock box, adding a custom (environmentally preferable) overlabel, and some savvy eye-grabbers from a scrapbook store. Very little investment required.

Glass and metals packaging.
The glass and metal industries are proud of their recycling rates, and, often, municipalities find recycling these materials to be a profit center rather than a drain on their budget, as regular trash removal is. These industries also enjoy good overall consumer perception and spend money on educational campaigns to encourage the consumer to recycle and buy recycled goods.

However, most glass and metals packaging industries have not felt it necessary to offer information about the recycled content of materials with any certainty for inclusion on package labels, as is done for paperboard (and now some plastics). Their collective stance has been that the process is too complex—blends of virgin and recycled materials vary batch by batch on the quality and availability of the ingredients at hand. Thus it is extremely difficult to track recycled content.

The plastics and paperboard industries face similar problems. But as examples in the book have shown, high post-consumer recycled plastic content disclosure is possible. If suppliers can be convinced to improve their materials accounting practices to tackle and track this recycled content, others should be able to as well.

Suppliers of glass or metals packaging are not usually the manufacturers of sheet steel/aluminum, or molders of glass. Because of this, the best way to find the right supplier/manufacturer is to review the industry Web sites (all offer lists of manufacturers/suppliers) and take the time to interview prospective vendors for their compatibility with your packaging goals. In addition, seek out vendors willing to tailor production to your specifications. Sometimes all that's needed to change an industry is for the customer to ask.

Resources

As soon as the ink dries on the printed pages of any resource directory, contact information inevitably changes. So in collaboration with designer Wendy Jedlicka, we've assembled a list of essential resources that often maintain their own databases and therefore should stand the test of time. Also thrown into the mix are a number of leading-edge material suppliers as well as wood reduction and environmental design resources from around the world. We hope this serves as a general primer on environmentally preferable packaging, one that prompts information, inspiration, and action.

MATERIALS TRADE ASSOCIATIONS AND RESEARCH ORGANIZATIONS

Metals and Glass

The Aluminum Association
Washington, DC
(202) 862-5100
www.aluminum.org
Industry group and Web site offering articles, statistics, and supplier and manufacturer resources.

American Iron and Steel Institute, Steel Packaging Council
Washington, DC
(202) 452-7100
www.steel.org
Industry group and Web site providing a good overview of how the steel industry works to increase efficiency. Use the links on this site to find vendors in your area.

Glass Packaging Institute
Alexandria, VA
(703) 684-6359
www.gpi.org
The Glass Packaging Institute maintains a member list that helps packaging designers locate vendors closest to their production area.

National Association of Aluminum Distributors
Philadelphia, PA
(215) 564-3484
Industry group and vendor locator. From cans to foil to laminates, aluminum provides a wide variety of both packaging solutions and packaging challenges.

Norsk GlassGjenvinning AS
Oslo, Norway
(+47) 23173980
www.glassgjenvinning.no
Industry Group and Web site listing manufacturers and suppliers of recycled glass and metals packaging and offering other information about European glass and metals recycling efforts.

Plastics—Recycled, Biobased, Degradable Blends

Association of Postconsumer Plastic Recyclers
Arlington, VA 22209
(703) 253-0605
Fax: (703) 253-0606
www.plasticsrecycling.org
Plastics recycling industry group and Web site offering background information about plastics recycling, a design guideline for working with recycled plastics, and member list to find fabricators in your area.

Biodegradable Plastics Society
www.bpsweb.net/02_english
Industry group and Web site.

Biodegradable Polymer Research Center
bprc.caeds.eng.uml.edu
Industry group and Web site.

Biodegradable Products Institute
New York, NY
(888) BPI-LOGO (274-5646)
www.bpiworld.org
Industry group and Web site list of certified biodegradable product manufacturers (mostly bags and films).

BioEnvironmental Polymer Society
Wyoming, MN
www.bedps.org
Industry group and Web site.

Biopolymer.net
www.biopolymer.net
Newsgroup and Web site. A comprehensive resource for manufacturers and buyers of bio-plastics and for those who want to keep abreast of this fast-changing field.

Recycled, Certified, Tree-Free Papers, Paperboard, and Molded Pulp

Alberta Research Council
Edmonton, Alberta, Canada
(780) 450-5111
www.arc.ab.ca
Leading research organization helping to develop and promote the use of nonwood fibers.

Certified Forest Products Council
Portland, OR
(503) 590-6600
www.certifiedwood.org
Industry group that promotes the Forest Stewardship Council, an independent, not-for-profit, voluntary initiative committed to promoting responsible forest products. Web site has a directory for certified sustainable wood and wood pulp suppliers.

Chlorine-Free Products Association
Algonquin, IL
(847) 658-6104
www.chlorinefreeproducts.org
Leading organization promoting and independently certifying manufacturers of paper, paperboard, molded pulp, and other products.

Forest Stewardship Council
Washington, DC
(202) 342-0413
www.fscus.org
Leading third-party certifier of ecological forest practices with over 100 million acres certified worldwide.

International Molded Pulp Environmental Packaging Association
Mequon, WI
(262) 241-0522
www.impepa.org
Industry group. Its Web site, though geared toward the molded-pulp professional, offers articles on technology developments, environmental legislation, current molded pulp products, and more. It does not provide a member list. To find a vendor in your area, write directly to the group.

100% Recycled Paperboard Alliance
Washington, DC
(315) 635-1215
www.rpa100.com
A great place to find suppliers and converters of 100 percent recycled paperboard packaging.

USDA Western Regional Resource Center
Albany, CA
(510) 559-5730
www.pw.usda.gov
Conducts research and develops technologies with companies to make use of agricultural fibers in paper, plastics, and other materials.

MANUFACTURERS AND SUPPLIERS

Adhesives

EcoSynthetix
Lansing, MI
(517) 336-4649
www.ecosynthetix.com
Biobased adhesive manufacturer. Offers a wide variety of degradable and benin adhesives suited to the challenge of packaging and print applications.

National Starch and Chemical Company
Bridgewater, NJ
(800) 797-4992
www.nationalstarch.com
Manufacturer of expanded starch-foam loose-fill peanuts and natural polymer adhesives.

Paper, Paperboard, and Molded-Pulp

Brodrene Hartmann
Lyngby, Denmark
(+45) 4587-5030
www.hartmann.dk
Manufacturer of post-consumer molded-pulp packaging for numerous applications.

Custom Paper Tubes
Cleveland, OH
(800) 766-2527
www.custompapertubes.com
Manufacturer of custom (and stock) recycled paper tubes.

Domtar Inc.
Montreal, Quebec, Canada
(514) 848-5400
Atlanta, GA
(404) 532-1140
www.domtar.com
One of the few manufacturers in North America producing a line of paper certified by the Forest Stewardship Council.

EnviroPak
St. Louis, MO
(314) 739-1202
www.enviropak.com
Manufacturer of molded-pulp packaging.

Georgia-Pacific Corporation
Atlanta, GA
(404) 652-4000
www.gp.com
Manufacturer of containerboard, converting papers, kraft papers, packaging, pulp, and recycled corrugated pallets. Containerboard and packaging converter.

Liberty Carton Company
Golden Valley, MN
(800) 328-1784
www.libertycarton.com
Innovative, privately owned manufacturer, printer, and supplier of containerboard, packaging, Point of Purchase, and retail (ready made) packaging from its own recycled paper mill.

New Leaf Paper
San Francisco, CA
(415) 291-9210
www.newleafpaper.com
Suppliers of high-PCR-content and FSC-certified papers.

Regale
Napa, CA
(707) 252-4818
www.regale.com
Suppliers of molded-pulp design and manufacturing systems. Working with communities around the world to establish mini-mills to make packaging from regional waste materials.

Ris Paper Company
Cincinnati, OH
(513) 244-2300
www.rispaper.com
Suppliers of FSC-certified papers.

Rock-Tenn Company
Norcross, GA
(770) 448-2193
www.rocktenn.com
100 percent recycled paperboard packaging manufacturer. High-volume printer, producing recycled paperboard packaging since 1908.

Plastics—Biodegradable, Biobased, and Conventional

AdalsonOY
Koria, Finland
(+35) 85886 5526
Manufacturer of molded-pulp packaging from flax and hemp fibers.

Biocorp North America
Los Angeles, CA
(310) 491-3465
www.biocorpaavc.com
Bioplastic packaging manufacturer.

Bioplastics Polymers and Composites
Lansing, MI
(303) 265-9072
Contact: narayan@msu.edu

Cargill Dow LLC
Minnetonka, MN
(877) 423-7659
www.cargilldow.com
Manufacturer of bio-plastic films, fibers, and polymers for packaging, textiles, and fiber fill.

Convex Plastics
Hamilton, New Zealand
(+64) 7 847 5133
www.convex.co.nz
Recycled polyethylene, flexible, ready-made bags and films.

DuPont Packaging and Industrial Polymers
Wilmington, DE
(877) 738-9537

EarthShell
Lutherville, MD
(410) 847-9420
www.earthshell.com
Manufacturer of food-service packaging. 100 percent biodegradable and recyclable through composting.

Earthware Biodegradables
(800) 211-6747
www.earthwarebiodegrad ables.com

Manufacturers of biodegradable disposable cutlery made from nongenetically engineered wheat and corn.

Eastman Chemical
Kingsport, TN
(800) 327-8626
www.eastman.com
Manufacturers of biobased plastics.

EMIUM
Buenos Aires, Argentina
(+5411) 4822-6362
www.emium.com.ar
Manufacturers of award-winning plastic bottles designed to interlock.

Enak
West Sussex,
United Kingdom
(+44) 0-1403-265544
www.enak.co.uk
Manufacturer of water-soluble plastic films.

Free-Flow Packaging
Redwood City, CA
(800) 866-9946
(650) 261-5300
www.fpintl.com
Recycles EPS, which is then reprocessed and used to create loose-fill packaging.

Kaufman Container
Minneapolis, MN
(612) 331-8880
www.kaufmancontainer.com
Distributor of plastic and glass containers with high post-consumer recycled content.

Metabolix
Cambridge, MA

(617) 492-0505
www.metabolix.com
Developers of polyhydroxy-buterate bioplastics primarily for medical applications.

Mitsubishi Gas and Chemical
New York, NY
(212) 752-4620

Novamont
Novara, Italy
(+39) 0321 699602
www.novamont.com

Pak-Sel, Inc.
Portland, OR
(503) 771-9404
www.cellobag.com
Converter and supplier of cellophane bags and films. Great short-run solution for wet items, fresh fruits, and vegetables, or as a replacement for polybags.

Paper Foam
Barneveld, The Netherlands
(+31) 0-342-401-667
www.paperfoam.com
Manufacturer of molded pulp that combines plant starch and recycled paper.

Potatopak Ltd.
Somerset, United Kingdom
(+44) 0 1963-362744
www.potatoplates.com
Manufacturers of potato-starch packaging and waterproof biodegradable trays.

Printers

Alonzo Printing
Hayward, CA
(800) 359-0522

(510) 293-3940
www.alonzoprinting.com
Printer (digital and offset), bindery, and mailing services. The first printer in Alameda County, California, to be certified as a Green Business.

Greg Barber Company
New York, NY
(516) 413-9207
www.gregbarberco.com
Print, book, and packaging printer. One of the few printers to feature tree-free packaging as well as 100 percent post-consumer content packaging.

Reusable Containers

CHEP
Orlando, FL
(888) 243-7111
www.chep.com
International suppliers of reusable pallets and container pools.

International Food Container Organization
Munich, Germany
(+49) 089-744-91-172
www.ifco.de
Distributes, collects, and redistributes reusable plastic containers in a cost-effective, sanitary manner to locations worldwide.

Rehrig Pacific
Los Angeles, CA
(800) 421-6244
www.rehrigpacific.com
International supplier of reusable plastic containers for foods and beverages.

Transport and Shock-Absorbing Packaging

Liberty Diversified Industries
New Hope, MN
(763) 536-6600
(800) 421-1270
Manufacturer of naturally pest-resistant recycled corrugated pallets, transport packaging, and reusable packaging.

Nippon Hi-Pack
Kasugai City, Japan
(+81) 56 834-8171
Hong Kong
(+852) 2730-1108
Manufacturers of recyclable fiberboard pallets made from post-consumer pulp.

Nuform Packaging
Tisdale, Saskatchewan, Canada
(306) 873-5505
www.nuformpkg.com
Producers of reusable transport and molded-pulp packaging for produce and other goods.

Orcon Industries
LeRoy, NY
(585) 768-7000
www.orconind.com
Manufactures 100 percent recycled paperboard thermoformed pulp packaging. Also fabricates and distributes packaging used for closed-loop returnable systems.

Packaging Corporation of America
Lake Forest, IL
(800) 456-4725
Fax: (847) 482-4545
www.packagingcorp.com
Manufacturer of recycled corrugated pallets. Not only are these pallets recycled but they are also recyclable.

Pro-Pac
Marrickville, Australia
(+61) 2 9560 7799
Manufacturers of loose-fill starch-based pellets.

RSVP Packaging
Campbell, CA
(408) 376-3877
www.rsvppkg.com
Manufacturers of shock-absorbing packaging systems that can be made with high post-consumer-content plastics.

Sealed Air
Danbury, CT
(203) 791-3559
www.sealedair.com
Manufacturers of shock-absorbing reusable packaging systems that significantly reduce amounts of necessary materials.

Sol Plastics
Montreal, Quebec, Canada
(888) SOL-PLAS (765-7527)
(514) 254-8525
www.solplastics.com
Manufacturer of 100 percent recycled plastic pallets. Its Web site boasts "We recycle more than 65 millions pounds (30,000 metric tons) of post-consumer and post-industrial waste a year."

Sonoco
Hatsville, SC
(800) 377-2692
www.sonoco.com
Producers of high post-consumer-content recycled-paper packaging materials.

StarchTech, Inc.
Golden Valley, MN
(612) 545-5400
www.starchtech.com
Manufacturer of expanded starch-foam, static-free, loose-fill peanuts.

NONGOVERNMENTAL ORGANIZATIONS

Packaging Organizations

Association of Packaging Technology and Research
Helsinki, Finland
(+09) 6162-3500
www.pyr.fi
Leading Web site from the Finnish Packaging Institute, the country with the lowest per capita disposable waste in Europe.

The European Organization for Packaging and the Environment
Brussels, Belgium
(+32) 2 736 3600
www.europen.be
Cross-discipline information source for sustainable packaging in the European Union. This Web site is the starting place for information on packaging laws or vendors in Europe.

Institute of Packaging Professionals
Naperville, IL
(630) 544-5050
Fax: (630) 544-5055
www.iopp.org
Industry group strives to help the industry develop in an environmentally responsible and economically viable way.

Packaging Association of Canada
Toronto, Ontario, Canada
(416) 490-7860
Fax: (416) 490-7844
www.pac.ca
One of the better Web sites offering information about the new Canadian packaging laws. It also has an easy-to-use vendor locator.

The University of York/ Friendly Packaging
Department of Biology
York, U.K.
(+44) 01-423-331-023
www.friendlypackaging.org.uk/index.htm
Web-based resource providing a good overview of current packaging plastics and packaging in general.

Leading Environmental Groups

Bioneers/Cultural Heritage Institute
Lamy, NM
(877) 246-6337
www.bioneers.org
Providing practical environmental solutions and innovative social strategies through

various media and annual conferences.

Canadian Markets Initiative
Torfino, British Columbia, Canada
(250) 725-2950
www.marketsinitiative.org
Home of the Canadian ancient-forest-friendly publishing campaign.

Conservatree
San Francisco, CA
(415) 721-4230
www.conservatree.com
Leading clearinghouse providing up-to-date supplier lists of recycled, certified, tree-free, and chlorine-free paper products and launching campaigns for environmentally preferable paper purchasing.

Environmental Defense/ Alliance for Environmental Innovation
Boston, MA
(617) 723-2996
www.environmentaldefense. org/alliance
Helps businesses create innovative, equitable, and cost-effective solutions to urgent environmental problems with manufacturing and packaging assessments. Web-based reference and white papers.

Environmental Paper Network
www.environmentalpaper.org
Coalition of numerous non-profit groups with programs to increase the use of environmentally preferable papers.

Grass Roots Recycling Network
Madison, WI
(608) 255-4800
www.grrn.org
Nonprofit that serves as a clearinghouse and promoter of extended producer responsibilty, zero waste, and regional resourcefulness.

GreenBlue/Sustainable Packaging Coalition
Charlottesville, VA
(434) 817-1424
www.greenblue.org
www.sustainablepackaging. org
Nonprofit organization focused on cradle-to-cradle design principles. The Sustainable Packaging Coalition is a collaboration of industry leaders working to create deep environmental packaging reform.

Institute for Agriculture and Trade Policy
Minneapolis, MN
(612) 870-0453
www.iatp.org
Nonprofit organization that works to promote sustainable agriculture and forestry both in the Midwest and internationally.

Institute for Local Self-Reliance
Minneapolis, MN
Washington, DC
(612) 379-3815
www.carbohydrateeconomy. org

Clearinghouse providing information on plant-matter-based products and leading biobased policy and research.

International Institute for Environment and Development
London, U.K.
(+44) 20 7388-2117
www.iied.org/smg/pubs/ rethink.html
"Rethinking Paper Consumption: A Discussion Paper," by Nick Robins and Sarah Roberts. Commissioned by the Norway Ministry of Environment as part of the OECD's program on sustainable production and consumption.

Our Stolen Future
www.ourstolenfuture.org
Leading clearinghouse of information on endocrine-disrupting chemicals furthering the work of the book by the same title.

Population Connection
Washington, DC
(202) 332-2200
www.populationconnection. org
Programs, resources, and education on the impacts of overpopulation.

Rainforest Action Network
San Francisco, CA
(415) 398-4404
www.ran.org
An organization that works internationally to preserve remaining intact temperate

and tropical forest ecosystems. Conducts campaigns to bring corporations into compliance with forest stewardship.

ReThink Paper
c/o Earth Island Institute
San Francisco, CA
(415) 788-3666 ext. 232
www.rethinkpaper.org
Web site offers lists of printers, paper suppliers, and mills as well as information on environmental laws, conservation issues, and trade associations.

Rocky Mountain Institute
Snowmass, CO
(970) 927-3851
www.rmi.org
Entrepreneurial organization fostering the efficient and restorative use of resources.

Sustainable Packaging Alliance
Victoria, Australia
www.sustainablepack.org
Initiative of Victoria University to research and help develop sustainable packaging systems by working with raw material manufacturers, converters, end users, retailers, collectors, and reprocessors.

Watershed Media
Healdsburg, CA
(707) 431-2936
www.watershedmedia.org
Leading publisher of professional resource tools on wood reduction, green design, sustainable agriculture, and more.

World Resources Institute
Washington, DC
(202) 729-7600
www.wri.org
Tracks leading indicators of
forest health, including The
Last Frontier Forests.

Sustainable Business Organizations

Businesses for Social Responsibility
San Francisco, CA
(415) 984-3200
www.bsr.org
Leading membership organ-
ization advocating the adoption of high standards for
environmentally, socially,
and economically sound
business practices.

The Center for Environmental Leadership in Business
www.celb.org
Established by Conservation
International and the Ford
Motor Company to promote
private sector solutions to
critical global issues.

Green Seal
Washington, DC
(202) 872-6400
www.greenseal.org
Independent green certification board.

***In Business* Magazine**
Emmaus, PA
(610) 967-4135 ext. 22
*www.jgpress.com/inbusine.
htm*
Magazine focusing on envi-
ronmental-minded market-

ing, technology, and growth
strategies.

Natural Capital Institute
Sausalito, CA
(415) 331-6241
www.naturalcapital.org
Home of a working group on
ecological business solutions
furthering the work of the
book *Natural Capitalism.*

OTHER PACKAGING-RELATED RESEARCH AND RESOURCES

Design Resources

Biomimicry Guild
Ada, MI
(616)560-8220
Helena, MT
(406) 495-1858
www.biomimicry.org
Consults with communities
and companies to create products, policies, and processes
that are inspired by and compatible with wild nature.

Celery Design Collaborative
Berkeley, CA
(510) 649-7155
www.celerydesign.com
Celery Design's "Ecological
Guide to Paper" references
only high post-consumer-
content, tree-free fiber, and
chlorine-free papers.

Independent Designers Network
Roseville, MN
(651) 636-0964
www.indes.net
Web-based reference offering
information on print, packag-

ing, materials, marketing,
and wastestream issues.

O2-USA
www.o2-usa.org
U.S. chapter of o2 Global Network. Both national and individual subchapter Web sites
provide a wide variety of reference links covering the big
picture of ecodesign as well
as more specific design topics.

Marketing Issues

Ethical Consumer
Manchester, U.K.
(+44) 0-161-226-2929
www.ethicalconsumer.org
Web site and consumer
activist group. Understanding the consumer is the heart
of effective packaging and
the key to market greening.

GreenBiz
www.greenbiz.com
An online journal of environmentally proactive business
practices.

LOHAS Journal
Broomfield, CO
(303) 222-8250
www.lohasjournal.com
Green business magazine
focusing on LOHAS
(Lifestyles of Health and Sustainability); it describes a
$226.8 billion U.S. market-
place for goods and services.

J. Ottman Consulting
New York, NY
(212) 255-3800
www.greenmarketing.com
Green-marketing consul-
tancy and online resource

helping businesses find
avenues for eco-innovation.

Life-Cycle Analysis

Alliance for Environmental Innovation
Boston, MA
(617) 723-2996
*www.environmentaldefense.
org/alliance*
Offers excellent studies on
packaging systems as well as
the Merge software that helps
perform life-cycle analyses
on packaging. Available free
with one-day training.

Imagination
United Kingdom
(+44) 20-7-628-0992
www.totalbeauty.org
A nonprofit foundation with
the aim of training a million
people in Datschefski's
cyclic/solar/safe design
methodology.

Scientific Certification Systems
www.scscertified.com
Independent certifier of
many kinds of products,
including Forest Steward-
ship Council virgin-wood
and post-consumer recycled-
content plastics.

Tellus Institute
Boston, MA
(617) 426-5844
www.tellus.org

University of Michigan, Center for Sustainable Systems
Ann Arbor, MI
(734) 764-1412

www.css.snre.umich.edu
Life-cycle analyses on packaging materials and systems.

Packaging Magazines

Packaging World Magazine, Summit Publishing Company
Chicago, IL
(312) 222-1010
www.packworld.com/cds_buyers.html
Web site that maintains a general directory of cross-industry packaging suppliers and manufacturers.

Stagnito Communications Inc.
Deerfield, IL
(847) 205-5660
www.stagnito.com
Packaging-industry magazine publisher. One of the best places to monitor mainstream packaging trends and alternative technologies breaking into the mainstream.

Packaging Legislation Information

Environmental Packaging International
Providence, RI
(401) 423-2225
www.enviro-pac.com
Consultancy group that helps companies large and small navigate the ever-changing environmental packaging regulations.

Environmental Protection Agency
Washington, DC
www.epa.gov/epr/products/packaging.html
An indispensible tool for understanding the maze of governmental initiatives regarding packaging.

Keller and Heckman
Washington, DC
(202) 434-4100
www.packaginglaw.com
Packaging lawyers. This Web site delivers clear and navigable information on often confusing packaging regulations. It also provides free monthly articles dealing with the ever-changing nuances of packaging law.

Raymond Communications
College Park, MD
(301) 345-4237
www.raymond.com
The subscription-based *Recycling Laws International* tracks up-to-date changes in packaging and recycling laws around the world. Hosts annual conferences on changing packaging laws and trends.

Printers and Information on Printing

Partners in Design
Seattle, WA
(206) 223-0681
www.pidseattle.com
Good source on toxics and heavy metals in inks. Also available are "EcoStrategies for Printed Communications:

An Information and Strategy Guide," a downloadable PDF guide detailing eco-printing strategies.

Printer's National Environmental Assistance Center
www.pneac.org
The PNEAC mission is to deliver current, reliable environmental compliance and pollution prevention information to printers, publishers, and packagers. A truly fantastic resource for anyone putting ink to paper.

Sustainable Purchasing

Center for a New American Dream
Takoma Park, MD
(301) 891-ENUF (3683)
www.newdream.org
www.ibuydifferent.org
Devoted to "helping Americans consume responsibly to protect the environment, enhance quality of life, and promote social justice."

Solid Waste Management Coordinating Board
www.swmcb.org/EPPG
Web site for the "Environmentally Preferable Purchasing Guide."

Transport Packaging

Minnesota Office of Environmental Assistance
Saint Paul, MN
(800) 657-3843
www.moea.state.mn.us/berc/transpac.cfm
"Transport Packaging Strategy" (a downloadable PDF)

is a tool to help large waste generators make informed decisions about reducing, reusing, and recycling transport packaging.

Reusable Transport Packaging Market Research Report
www.swmcb.org/studies Marketresearchreport.html
Focuses on the factors of reusable transport packaging.

Solid Waste Management Coordinating Board
www.swmcb.org/studies
Offers reports on reusable transport packaging.

Waste Issues

EPA/WasteWise
www.epa.gov
www.epa.gov/wastewise
A free, voluntary, EPA program helping U.S. organizations eliminate costly municipal solid waste, benefiting the bottom line and the environment. Scroll to Environmentally Preferable Purchasing Program.

Natural Resources Defense Council
New York, NY
(212) 727-2700
www.nrdc.org/cities/recycling/default.asp
Helps communities solve pressing needs, like turning recycling programs from budget sinks into profit centers.

NOTES

1. William McDonough and Michael Braungart, "The Next Industrial Revolution," Atlantic Monthly, October 1998, pp. 82–92.

2. John Winter and Anne Marie Alonso, *Waste at Work: Prevention Strategies for the Bottom Line* (New York: INFORM, 1999).

3. Jim Motavalli, "Zero Waste," E Magazine, March/April 2001, p. 31.

4. "Greener Cartons: A Buyer's Guide to Recycled-Content Paperboard," report, Alliance for Environmental Innovation, November 20, 2001.

5. Food Service and Packaging Institute, "Expected Time to Prepare a Meal," 1996.

6. Paul Hawken, Amory Lovins, and Hunter Lovins, *Natural Capitalism: Creating the Next Industrial Revolution* (New York: Back Bay Books, 2000), 52–53.

7. Xu Zhengfeng, "Putting an End to a Plastic Plague," *Asia Times*, August 17, 1999, www.atimes.com/china/AH17Ad02.html.

8. Lynn Scarlett, "Packaging and Environmental Policies—North America," in *Packaging, Policy, and the Environment*, edited by Geoffrey M. Lovy (New York: Aspen, 2000), 251.

9. Geoffrey M. Levy, "Introduction," in Levy, *Packaging, Policy, and the Environment*, 3.

10. Primo Angeli, *Making People Respond: Design for Marketing and Communication* (New York: Madison Square Press, 1996), 11.

11. From the Food Marketing Institute, cited in Mary K. Schmidl, "A Vision of Food in the 21st Century," Western Knight Center for Specialized Journalism, U.C. Berkeley Graduate School of Journalism, Food and Environment Conference, September 23, 2002.

12. Frank Ackerman, "Environmental Impacts of Packaging in the U.S. and Mexico," *Society for Philosophy and Technology* 2, no. 2 (Winter 1997).

13. Rich Pirog and Tim Van Pelt, "Food, Fuel, and Freeways," report for Leopold Center for Sustainable Agriculture, Iowa State University, April 19, 2002.

14. Jim Butschi, *Packaging World Magazine*, September 2002, p. 156, Web version.

15. Hawken et al., *Natural Capitalism*, 52.

16. Gary Polavic, "Report Finds More Emissions Caused by Energy Exploration," *San Jose Mercury News*, October 7, 2003.

17. Alan Hershkowitz, *Bronx Ecology: Blueprint for a New Environmentalism.* (Washington, D.C.: Island Press, 2002), 64.

18. Ibid.

19. Christopher Wells, "Packaging and Environmental Policies—Brazil," 379, and Hifrofumi Miki and Yoshio Oki, "Packaging and Environmental Policies—Japan," 337, both in Levy, *Packaging, Policy, and the Environment*.

20. Edward Denison and Guang Yu Ren, *Thinking Green: Packaging Prototypes 3* (Hove, East Sussex: RotoVision, 2001), 42.

21. John C. Ryan and Alan Thien Durning, *Stuff: The Secret Life of Everyday Things* (Seattle: Northwest Environmental Watch, 1997), 37.

22. Ibid., 38.

23. "Council of State Governments/Tellus Packaging Study: Report #5: Executive Summary," Tellus Institute, May 1992, p. 26.

24. Thomas Hine, *The Total Package: The Evolution and Secret Meanings of Boxes, Bottles, Cans, and Tubes* (Boston: Little, Brown, 1995), 248.

25. Wendell Berry, "The Whole Horse: The Preservation of the Agrarian Mind," *Fatal Harvest: The Tragedy of Industrial Agriculture* (Washington, D.C.: Island Press, 2002), 7–11.

26. Denison and Yu Ren, *Thinking Green*, 14; Elaine Barrett and Jane Bickerstaffe, "Packaging's Role in Society," in Levy, *Packaging, Policy, and the Environment*, 61–63.

27. T. Slowe, "Extended Producer Responsibility and the Problem of Packaging Waste," *United States Technology, Industry, and Ecology*, December 2001, p. 4.

28. Chris Smith and Peter White, "Life Cycle Assessment of Packaging," in Levy, *Packaging, Policy, and the Environment*, 196.

29. Katherine M. Flegal et al., "Prevalance and Trends in Obesity Among U.S. Adults, 1999–2000," *Journal of the American Medical Association* 288, no. 14 (October 2002).

30. Michael Pollan, "The Way We Live Now: The (Agri)Cultural Contradictions of Obesity," *New York Times Magazine*, October 12, 2003.

31. Presentation by Eric Schlosser at the Western Knight Center for Specialized Journalism, U.C. Berkeley Graduate School of Journalism, Food and Environment Conference, September 23, 2002.

32. Schmidl, "A Vision of Food in the 21st Century."

33. Aaron Brody, presentation at the Conference on Food and the Environment, University of California at Berkeley, Graduate School of Journalism, September 2002.

34. Edwin Datschefski, *The Total Beauty of Sustainable Products* (Hove, East Sussex: RotoVision, 2001), 23.

35. William McDonough and Michael Braungart, *Cradle to Cradle: Remaking the Way We Make Things* (New York: North Point Press, 2002), 61.

36. David Wann, "Waste Makes Haste," *AlterNet*, June 16, 2003, www.alternet.org/storyhtml?StoryID=16173.

37. European Environment Agency, European Union, *Environmental Signals 2002: Waste and Material Flows* (accessed August 2, 2002), http://themes.eea.eu.int/Environmental_issues/waste/indicators.

38. Scarlett, "Packaging and Environmental Policies—North America," 255.

39. Ibid.

40. Rod Miller, phone interview, October 2000, cited in Daniel Imhoff, "Thinking Outside the Box," *Whole Earth* (Winter 2002): 10.

41. "Council of State Governments/Tellus Packaging Study: Report #5: Executive Summary," Tellus Institute, May 1992, p. 9.

42. Ackerman, "Environmental Impacts of Packaging."

43. "Paper Task Force Recommendations for Purchasing and Using Environmentally Preferable Paper: Final Report," Environmental Defense Fund, 1995.

44. DoE Energy Information Administration, "Measuring Energy Efficiency in the United States' Economy: A Beginning," chap. 5: Transportation Sector, fig. 5-21 (www.eia.doe.gov/emeu/efficiency/ee_ch5.htm).

45. Mike Brown, phone interview, November 16, 2004.

46. Carl Rabago, phone interviews and email exchanges, Fall 2003.

47. Maude Barlow and Tony Clarke, *Blue Gold: The Fight to Stop the Corporate Theft of the World's Water* (New York: New Press, 2002), 142.

48. Interview on KQED Forum, Friday, June 6, 2003, with Californians Against Waste.

49. Barlow and Clarke, *Blue Gold*.

50. Cited in ibid.

51. Hershkowitz, *Bronx Ecology*, 58.

52. Ibid., 144.

53. Maude Barlow, plenary presentation at Bioneers 14th Annual Conference, San Rafael, California, October 17, 2003.

54. David Newcorn, "Packagers React to Cradle-to-Cradle Design," *Packaging World Magazine*, May 3, 2003, p. 70, http://packworld.com/cds_print.html?rec_id=16104.

55. Denison and Yu Ren, *Thinking Green*, 28.

56. Ibid., 29.

57. Arne Naess, "Deep Ecology for the Twenty-Second Century," in *Deep Ecology for the 21st Century: Readings on the Philosophy and Practice of the New Environmentalism*, edited by George Sessions (Boston: Shambhala, 1995), 463.

58. Newcorn, "Packagers React to Cradle-to-Cradle Design." Newcorn's survey showed that, though 88 percent of packaging professionals would personally support "cradle to cradle" environmental packaging initiatives, only 50 percent believed their companies would support them.

59. U.S. EPA Office of Solid Waste and Emergency Response, *Municipal Solid Waste in the United States: 2000 Facts and Figures*, June 2002, p. 78; European Environment Agency, European Union, *Environmental Signals 2002: Waste and Material Flows* (accessed August 2, 2002), http://themes.eea.eu.int/Environmental_issues/waste/indicators.

60. Cogent mainstream critiques of economic globalization can be found in such books as Hawken et al., *Natural Capitalism*; Jerry Mander and Edward Goldsmith, *The Case Against the Global Economy* (San Francisco: Sierra Club Books, 1996); Lester Brown, *Eco-Economy: Building an Economy for the Earth* (New York: Norton, 2001); and Joel Kovel, *The Enemy of Nature: The End of Capitalism or the End of the World?* (London: Zed Books, 2002).

61. Monica Shaw, "Finding the Courage to Invest," *Pulp and Paper*, Paper Loop archive, 2001, www.paperloop.com/db_area/archive/p_pmag/2001/0007/editor.htm.

62. William Booth, "EPA Sets Recycling Goal," *Washington Post*, January 5, 2000, p. A3.

63. Bette K. Fishbein, "EPR: What Does It Mean, Where Is It Headed?" *P2 Pollution Prevention Review* 8 (1988), cited at www.mindfully.org/Sustainability-Extended-Producer-Responsibility.htm.

64. Anne Chick, phone interview.

65. Duales Systems Deutschland AG, *Annual Report, 1999*, p. 6.

66. Sara Bloom, "How Is Germany Dealing with Its Packaging Waste?" *Whole Earth* (Winter 2002): 23–24.

67. Ibid.

68. "New German Government Sticks to Recycling Law," Reuters News Service, October 14, 2002.

69. "German Drinks Industry Suspends Recycling Deal," Reuters News Service, June 5, 2003, online edition.

70. Michele Raymond, "Extended Producer Responsibility Laws: A Global Policy Analysis," Raymond Communications, www.environmental-center.com/articles/article 996/extended.pdf.

71. Ibid.

72. Jacques Fonteyne, "Packaging Recovery and Recycling Policy in Practice," in Levy, *Packaging, Policy, and the Environment*, 244.

73. Levy, "Introduction," 35.

74. Ibid.

75. Raymond, "Extended Producer Responsibility Laws."

76. Gary Volsen, Willamette Industries (now purchased by Weyerhauser), personal interview, 2001.

77. Margaret Papadakis, personal communication, Summer 2003, and phone interview, October 2, 2003.

78. Marissa Juhler, phone interview, June 2003.

79. Information in this case study comes primarily from "Finland's Reusable System" in Denison and Yu Ren, *Thinking Green*.

80. Tony Woods and David Benyon, "Managing the Environmental Impacts of Packaging Manufacture," in Levy, *Packaging, Policy, and the Environment*, 155.

81. "Best Bosses: Profiles," *Fortune Small Business* magazine, October 2003.

82. McDonough and Braungart, *Cradle to Cradle*, 45–67.

83. Information and quotations in this case study come from numerous phone interviews and some email exchanges with Hewlett-Packard employees. In particular, Kevin Howard, phone interview, October 2001.

84. Mary Tkach, phone interview.

85. "Wrap Artists: How Aveda Bundles Sustainability into Its Packaging," *The Green Business Letter*, December 2003, p. 6.

86. John Delfausse, personal communication, phone interviews, and email exchanges.

87. Andrea Ash, phone interviews.

88. "Ben and Jerry's Dioxin Controversy," Environmental News Service, August 18, 2000, www.wired.com/news/technology/0,1282,38302,00.html.

89. Dan Imhoff, "Victor Papanek in Memoriam," *Communications Arts*, May/June 1998, p. 130.

90. Michael Braungart, email correspondence.

91. Datschefski, *Total Beauty of Sustainable Products*, 29.

92. Ibid.

93. Hawken et al., *Natural Capitalism*, chap. 1, online edition at www.natcap.org/.

94. E. F. Schumacher, *Small Is Beautiful: Economics as if People Mattered* (New York: Harper and Row, 1973).

95. McDonough and Braungart were interviewed and their ideas discussed in David Newcorn, "Cradle-to Cradle: A New Packaging Paradigm?" *Packaging World*, May 2003.

96. For more information, see sustainablepackaging.org/ or greenblue.org/. Companies, organizations, and agencies with representatives in attendance so far include ALCOA, Cargill Dow, Coca-Cola, Darden School of Business Administration, Dow Chemical Company, DuPont, Esteé Lauder/Aveda, EvCo Research, Exopack, Masterfoods, Mead West-VaCa, Nike, PepsiCo, PMMI, Priority Metrics Group, Rocky Mountain Institute, Starbucks Coffee, Unilever, and the U.S. Environmental Protection Agency.

97. Anne Chick, personal communication.

98. Brian Dougherty, interviews and email exchanges.

99. R. Costanza, R. d'Arge, and R. de Groot, "The Value of the World's Ecosystem Services and Natural Capital," *Nature*, May 15, 1997, pp. 253–60.

100. "Fragmenting Forests: Loss of Large Frontier Forests," World Resources Program, 1988 89, earthtrends.wri.org/features/view_feature.cfm?theme=9&fid=14.

101. Alan Hershkowitz, *Bronx Ecology: Blueprint for a New Environmentalism* (Washington, D.C.: Island Press, 2002), 68.

102. See the Dogwood Alliance and World Resources Institute for more detailed information. Some useful Web sites include www.fscus.org/, www.oldgrowthfree.org/, www.wri.org/.

103. Tom Knudson, "State of Denial: World's Other Forests Feed State's Appetite for Timber," *Sacramento Bee*, October 5, 2003.

104. Hershkowitz, *Bronx Ecology*, 59.

105. "Changing Regulations on Packing Material: Will You Be Affected?" FAS Online, www.fas.usda.gov/info/agexporter/2001/jan/PackingRegulations.htm.

106. "Big City Forest Products Information Sheet" (New York, 1996), cited in Winter and Alonso, *Waste at Work*, 30.

107. Rick Weiss, "Study Finds Seeds Tainted with Engineered DNA Strands," *San Francisco Chronicle*, February 24, 2004, p. A2.

108. The Consumers Union Guide to ecolabels, www.eco-labels.org/.

109. "Minnesota Pallet Makers Serve Niche for Certified Wood Resource: Two Pallet Makers Respond to Environmental Concerns," *FSC Newsletter*, August 2003, pp. 2–3.

110. Dan Imhoff, "A Bright Sign: CFPA Makes Its Mark," *Communication Arts*, September–October 1998, p. 116.

111. The Worldwatch Institute, *State of the World 2000* (New York: W.W. Norton, 2000).

112. Chlorine-Free Products Association, "10 Ways to Impact," educational brochure.

113. Sandra Steingraber, "Illiopolis: Center of Disaster and Environmental Hazard," *Chicago Tribune*, May 4, 2004.

114. "Council of State Governments/Tellus Packaging Study: Report #5: Executive Summary," Tellus Institute, May 1992, p. 10.

115. Hawken et al., *Natural Capitalism*.

116. Gary Volsen, Willamette Industries (now purchased by Weyerhauser), phone interview, 2001.

117. National Pollutant Release Inventory, 1996, as cited on the Reach for Unbleached Web site, www.rfu.org/AboutPulp.htm; "Paper Task Force Recommendations for Purchasing and Using Environmentally Preferable Paper: Final Report," Environmental Defense Fund, 1995, p. 13; Janet N. Abramowivitz and Ashley Mattoon, "Paper Cuts: Recovering the Paper Landscape," Worldwatch Paper 149, Worldwatch Institute, December 1999, pp. 25–29.

118. Hershkowitz, *Bronx Ecology*, 253.

119. Steve Underwood, phone interview.

120. Greg Gale, interview, quoted in Dan Imhoff, "Space Age Egg Carton," *EcoNewsletter/Communication Arts* 10, no. 4 (June 2001): 129.

121. "Easy Come, Easy Go? Bioplastics Offer Great Promise, But Breaking Down Is Still Hard to Do," *The GreenBusiness Letter*, August 2002, p. 5.

122. Ibid.

123. Leslie Guttman, "In Search of the Perfect Clamshell," *Salon.com*, March 3, 2004/archive.salon.com/tech/feature/2004/03/eco_clamshell.

124. Charles Benbrook, "Seeds of Doubt," report, September 2002, www.alternativesante.com/download/soil_association_report.pdf

125. Elisabeth Malkin, "Mexico Is Warned of Risk from Altered Corn," *New York Times*, March 13, 2004, p. A5.

126. Michael Pollan, "When a Crop Becomes King," *New York Times*, July 19, 2002.

127. Tillman Gerngross, phone interview, September 11, 2003.

128. Tillman Gerngross and Steven Slater, "How Green Are Green Plastics?" *Scientific American*, August 20, 2000.

129. Ibid.

130. Tillman Gerngross, phone interview, September 11, 2003.

131. Gerngross and Slater, "How Green Are Green Plastics?"

132. Robert Leaversuch, "Biodegradable Polyesters: Packaging Goes Green," *Plastics Technology Online*, September 2002.

133. Karl Rabago, phone interview, September 11, 2003, and email correspondence.

134. David Abrams, *The Spell of the Sensuous: Perception and Language in a More Than Human World* (New York: Vintage, 1997), 268.

135. "Report of the Starbucks Coffee Company/Alliance for Environmental Innovation Joint Task Force," April 15, 2000, p. 8, www.environmentaldefense.org/pdf.cfm?ContentID-523&FileName=starbucks.pdf.

136. Amory Lovins, L. Hunter Lovins, and Marty Bender, "Energy and Agriculture," in *Meeting the Expectations of the Land*, edited by Wes Jackson, Wendell Berry, and Bruce Coleman (New York: North Point Press, 1984), 68.

137. "Measuring Food by the Mile," *Living Earth and the Food Magazine*, SAFE, www.mcspotlight.org/media/reports/food-miles.html.

138. Amy Satkofsky, "Matchmaking in New York City: Program Gives New Life to Materials Through an Innovative Management and Exchange Program," *In Business*, May/June 2002, pp. 28–29.

139. Ibid.

140. For more information, see http://wastematch.org/.

141. Ibid.

142. Steve Simmons, phone interview and radio interview, June 25, 2001. For more about the project, see "Students Build Owl Boxes to Restore Wildlife," in *California Vineyards and Wildlife Habitat* (Sacramento: California Association of Wine Grape Growers, 2003), 48–51.

143. "Consumers Urged to Slash Trash," Environmental News Network, April 9, 1999, www.enn.com/.

144. Jeannine Aversa, "Household Debt Levels OK, Greenspan Says," *San Francisco Chronicle*, February 25, 2004, p. B5.

145. Warren Karlenzig, personal communication.

146. Richard Farinelli, phone interview, September 2003.

Alliance for Environmental Innovation, "Greener Cartons: A Buyer's Guide to Recycled-Content Paperboard," November 20, 2001 (www.environmentaldefense.org/alliance/reports.html).

Angeli, Primo. *Making People Respond: Design for Marketing and Communication*. Boston: Madison Square Press, 1996.

Barlow, Maude, and Tony Clark. *Blue Gold: The Fight to Stop the Corporate Theft of the World's Water*. New York: New Press, 2002.

Benyus, Janine M. *Biomimicry: Innovation Inspired by Nature*. New York: Quill, 1997.

Brown, Lester. *Eco-Economy: Building an Economy for the Earth*. New York: W. W. Norton, 2001.

Brown, Lester, Jent Larsen, and Bernie Fischloz-Roberts. *The Earth Policy Reader*. New York: W. W. Norton, 2002.

Chick, Anne. *The Graphic Designer's Greenbook: Environmental Concerns of the Design and Print Industries*. Zurich: Graphis, 1992.

Datschefski, Edwin. *The Total Beauty of Sustainable Products*. Hove, East Sussex: RotoVision, 2001.

Denison, Edward, and Guang Yu Ren. *Thinking Green: Packaging Prototypes 3*. Hove, East Sussex: Roto Vision, 2001.

Falk, Robert. *The Use of Recycled Wood and Paper in Building Applications*. Madison, Wisc.: Forest Products Society, 1997.

Fishbein, Bette, John Ehrenfeld, and John Young. *Extended Producer Responsibility: A Materials Policy for the 21st Century*. New York: INFORM, 2000.

Fuad-Luke, Alastair. *Eco Design: The Sourcebook*. San Francisco: Chronicle Books, 2002.

Hawken, Paul, Amory Lovins, and Hunter Lovins. *Natural Capitalism: Creating the Next Industrial Revolution*. New York: Back Bay Books, 2000.

Hershkowitz, Allen. *Bronx Ecology: Blueprint for a New Environmentalism*. Washington, D.C.: Island Press, 2002.

Hine, Thomas. *The Total Package: The Evolution and Secret Meanings of Boxes, Bottles, Cans, and Tubes*. New York: Little, Brown, 1995.

Imhoff, Daniel. *Building with Vision: Optimizing and Finding Alternatives to Wood*. Healdsburg, Calif.: Watershed Media, 2001.

———. *The Guide to Tree-Free, Recycled, and Certified Papers*. Healdsburg Calif.: SimpleLife Books, 1999.

International Forum on Globalization. *Alternatives to Economic Globalization: A Better World Is Possible*. San Francisco: Berrett-Koehler, 2002.

———. *Intrinsic Consequences of Economic Globalization on the Environment*. Preliminary report. San Francisco, December 2002.

Kovel, Joel. *The Enemy of Nature: The End of Capitalism or the End of the World?* London: Zed Books, 2002.

Levy, Geoffrey M., editor. *Packaging, Policy, and the Environment*. New York: Aspen, 2000.

McDonough, William, and Michael Braungart. *Cradle to Cradle: Remaking the Way We Make Things*. New York: North Point Press, 2002.

Papanek, Victor. *Design for the Real World: Human Ecology and Social Change*. New York: Pantheon, 1971.

———. *The Green Design Imperitive: Natural Design for the Real World*. London: Thames and Hudson, 1995

Paper Task Force. *Paper Task Force Recommendations for Purchasing and Using Environmentally Preferable Paper: Final Report*. New York: The Environmental Defense Fund, 1995.

Pauli, Gunter. *Upsizing: The Road to Zero Emissions, More Jobs, More Income, and No Pollution*. Sheffield: Greenleaf Publishing, 1998.

Ryan, John, and Alan Thein Durning. *Stuff: The Secret Lives of Everyday Things*. Seattle: Northwest Environment Watch, 1997.

Schlosser, Eric. *Fast Food Nation: The Dark Side of the All-American Meal*. New York: Houghton Mifflin, 2001.

Sellen, Abigail, and Richard Harper. *The Myth of the Paperless Office*. Cambridge: MIT Press, 2002.

Food Routes, 120, 143
footprint, 14, 86, 129
Ford, Henry, 108
forest products industry: chlorine-bleaching and, 38, 64–65; clearcutting, 8, 80–81; and forestry practices, 8–9, 15, 23, 81; government subsidies and, 40–41; history and scope of, 80; industrial logging, 80–82; "junk trees," 85; rainforest protection, 88; reform, 45, 88–89. See also paper; paper industry; wood-based packaging
Forest Stewardship Council (FSC): certification, 45, 65, 89, 94–95, 131; certified wood pallets, 97, 134; and ecolabels, 92, 93; origins of, 95, 151; rival standards and, 95
Four Season Farm, 142
France, 47, 48, *50*
fresh produce packs, 130–31
FSC. See Forest Stewardship Council
Fuller, Buckminster, 66
functional food wraps, 137
function of packaging, 10–13, 34–35
future outlook; bioplastics, 113–14, 117; conscious choice and reform, 124–25; good wraps, 136–40; hyperprocessing, 20–21; integrated systems and "technical nutrients," 25; public awareness and change, 11, 35, 128–29; Regale's "township factories," 106–7; strategic and analytic processes, 28–29; technology and food packaging, 20–21. See also biomimicry; reform

gable-top carton, 132
Gale, Greg, 104, 106–7
genetically modified organisms (GMOs), 90, 109–11, 114
GeoCup, 139

Germany: and EPR laws, 42, 46–49; Green Dot system, 45–48; recycling rates, 40
Gerngross, Tillman, 112, 113
gift wrap, 10, 128–29
glass: beer bottles, 32–33, 53, 138; energy for manufacturing, *29*; recycling, 16, 24, 139; reusing, 32–33, 133, 138; source reduction and, 55; upstream consequences of, 16. See also beverage containers
global economy: biological threats, 22–23, 41, 43, 84, 134; bottled water, 29, 30; and global ignorance, 18; global waste trade, 41; natural systems design, 67; paperboard recycling, 15; predatory capitalism, 40; primary packaging, 12; transport and shipping, 13, 22–23, 28, 134–35. See also local/regional products
global warming, 18, 24, 35, 90
GMOs. See genetically modified organisms
Government Purchasing Project (GPP), 87
The Graphic Designer's Greenbook (Chick), 73
Grass Roots Recycling Network, 10
Great Depression, 108
green agriculture, 116, 120
green architecture, 67, 120
GreenBlue, 45, 72
The Green Design Imperative (Papanek), 67
Green Dot system, 46–48
"greener" boxboard project, 96
Green Party, 42, 46–47
"green purchasing" policies, 87–88

Hammond, Bruce, 96
Hawken, Paul, 10, 14, 71–72
Hayes, Randy, 6–7
heavy metals. See toxins
Heineken, Alfred, 32–33

Hershkowitz, Allen, 30, 82, 101
Hewlett-Packard, 58–59, 105, 106
Hicks, Michael, 83
Hine, Thomas, 17
Home Depot, 84
Howard, Kevin, 58–59
Huhtamaki, 99
Huta, Leda, 80
hyper-processing, 20–21

IKEA, 142
impact assessment. See LCA
In Business (magazine), 121
Independent Designers Network, 149
individual ecology, 35, 128–30
individual packaging materials/systems, 130–35
industrial agriculture, 116–17, 134
industrial logging, 80–82
Industrial Revolution, 71
industry trade groups, 92, 94–95
INFORM, 46
information-intensive packaging, 127
infrastructure development, 39, 113
inks, 74–75, 114, 134, 139
Inman, Mark, 142
innovative packaging, 136–45
Institute of Environmental Health Sciences, 98
integrated infrastructure development, 39, 113
integration. See whole systems approach
international reform: empty-space laws, 42; European Union, 36, 43, 47–48; France and the 3Rs, 47; legislation in Europe, 36; moratoriums, 44, 49, 108, 128. See also EPR laws
Internet product delivery, 44, 86
intra-industry standardization, 39

"Intrinsic Environmental Consequences of Trade-Related Transport" (Mander and Retallack), 22–23
isosorbide, 109–10

Japan: aluminum recycling in, 15; bioplastics, 109, 115; community-supported agriculture and, 119; empty-space laws, 42; EPR laws in, 49, *50*; packaging reform in, 43, 130
Jedlicka, Wendy, 149
Johnson, Tim, 139
Journal of the American Medical Association, 20
Juhler, Marissa, 52
"junk species," 85

Korea, 70. See also South Korea
Kyoto Protocol, 43

labels: ecolabels, 45, 91–95; information-intensive packaging, 127; inks, 74–75, 114, 134, 139; label-less branding, 136, 138; solutions for, 149; SoySeal trademark label, 74
landfills, 25, 42, 44
Latin America, 31
laws. See policy
LCA. See life-cycle analysis/assessment
Leahy, Patrick, 87
Leopold Center for Sustainable Agriculture, 13
life-cycle analysis/assessment (LCA): biases and limitations of, 27, 28; corn and bioplastic production, 112–13, 116–17; of individual packaging materials, 13, 130–35; lightweighting and, 55–56; and natural systems designs, 43–45, 68; whole systems approach and, 29

Daniel Imhoff is a writer, publisher, and speaker on issues related to food, agriculture, forestry, and design. He is the author of numerous articles, essays, and books, including *Farming with the Wild* (2003), *Building with Vision* (2001), *Fat Tire: A Celebration of the Mountain Bike* (1999), and *The Guide to Tree-Free, Recycled, and Certified Papers* (1999). Dan is co-founder of Watershed Media, a Northern California–based nonprofit organization that produces and publishes resources designed to catalyze awareness and inspire direct action around urgent issues. He received a B.A. in International Relations from Allegheny College and an M.A. in International Affairs from the Maxwell School of Public Affairs at Syracuse University. He lives with his wife and two children; they divide their time between Healdsburg and a small homestead farm in California's Anderson Valley.

Roberto Carra, principal photographer for *Paper or Plastic* and co-founder of Watershed Media, is an internationally renowned photographer, graphic designer, and art director. His still-life photography for the Esprit image studio during the 1980s and 1990s significantly influenced commercial communication. A classically trained graphic artist, Carra works in a broad range of visual communication media. He is a widely published editorial photographer as well as an art director whose work appears in books and magazines throughout the world. He currently lives and works in northern Italy.

Watershed Media is an award-winning communications organization that produces strategically tailored projects to catalyze change around urgent and often under-reported environmental issues. Watershed Media was founded by a research, writing, and graphic design team who have been collaborating on environmental and social issues communications topics for over a decade and who believe that visually dynamic, concisely written, audience-specific tools can not only increase education but also influence behavior in moving us toward a more sustainable society.

Watershed Media
451 Hudson Street
Healdsburg, CA 95448
www.watershedmedia.org
(707) 431-2936